D0819809

POPULAR AMERICAN COMPOSERS

FROM REVOLUTIONARY TIMES TO THE PRESENT

FIRST SUPPLEMENT

A Biographical and Critical Guide

Compiled and Edited by
DAVID EWEN

With an Index of Songs, Productions, and Record Albums

THE H. W. WILSON COMPANY
NEW YORK   1972

POPULAR AMERICAN COMPOSERS

FIRST SUPPLEMENT

Copyright © 1972
By The H. W. Wilson Company
First Printing 1972
Second Printing 1976

———

Printed in the United States of America
International Standard Book Number 0-8242-0436-0

Library of Congress Catalog Card

INTRODUCTION

Popular American Composers, published in 1962, was the first such biographical guide to the principal American popular composers. This volume is its supplement. It updates the biographies of those composers represented in the earlier volume who have remained productive and includes thirty-one new biographies of composers who have come into prominence since 1962. With minor exceptions most of the material for these new biographies was acquired from first-hand sources (the composers themselves) or from reliable secondary sources (their personal representatives or publishers). This is also true of the updated material in biographies of composers previously represented.

Some of the new biographies are of composers who have made important contributions to the Broadway musical theater, motion pictures, and the commercial popular song. But most of the new entries concern those who have emerged since 1962 as the foremost exponents of rock 'n' roll, country and western music, and other new styles that have dominated popular music since the late 1950's. In 1962, when Popular American Composers was first published, it was still too soon to give proper perspective to the work then being done in the new areas of popular music. It was too soon to distinguish those composers of the new styles whose creativity would be sustained beyond two or three hits or whose influence would be far reaching and lasting. It is possible to do so now.

The editor has found it convenient throughout the text to use those abbreviations, nicknames, or terms which have entered the permanent vocabulary of our popular music. Oscar represents the award of the Academy of Motion Picture Arts and Sciences; Grammy, that of the National Academy of Recording Arts and Sciences; and Emmy, that of the Academy of Television Arts and Sciences. ASCAP represents the American Society of Composers, Publishers and Authors, and BMI, Broadcast Music, Inc. A gold disk or album is one that has sold one million copies or more. Top ten refers to the ten leading record sellers of the week on the best-seller charts compiled by leading record trade and other journals.

David Ewen

Miami, Florida

CONTENTS

Necrology

Deaths reported since the first printing of POPU-
LAR AMERICAN COMPOSERS: FIRST SUPPLEMENT in 1972

Leroy Anderson   May 18, 1975

Shelton Brooks   September 6, 1975

Bobby Darin   December 20, 1973

Duke Ellington   May 24, 1974

Rudolf Friml   November 12, 1972

Harry Ruby February 23, 1974

POPULAR AMERICAN COMPOSERS

FIRST SUPPLEMENT

Richard Adler 1921-

For biographical sketch and list of earlier songs see *Popular American Composers,* 1962.

———

Although Richard Adler's Broadway musical *Kwamina* (1961) was a failure, its score yielded two excellent songs: the the opening number, "The Cocoa Bean Song," and the principal love ballad, "Another Time, Another Place." The latter was popularized on records and over television by Robert Goulet. In both songs Adler was his own lyricist.

Adler's next musical, *A Mother's Kisses,* for which he wrote his own lyrics, was also a failure. It opened and closed out of town in 1968. Before that, in 1966, he had written the words and music for an American Broadcasting Company television special, *Olympus 7-1000,* which he also produced.

In 1963 Adler produced and directed the Inaugural Anniversary Salute to President John F. Kennedy in Washington, D.C. A year later he was director and master of ceremonies for the first state dinner entertainment of President Johnson's Administration. Between 1965 and 1969 Adler was consultant on the arts for the White House. He has also been consultant on the arts to the governor of North Carolina and has served on the advisory board of the School of Performing Arts in North Carolina.

Adler was divorced from Sally Ann Howes, the actress, in 1966. On December 27, 1968, he married Ritchey Banker. They make their home in an apartment in New York City.

Milton Ager 1893-

See *Popular American Composers,* 1962.

Fred Ahler 1892-1953

See *Popular American Composers,* 1962.

Louis Alter 1902-

For biographical sketch and list of earlier songs see *Popular American Composers,* 1962.

———

Between 1964 and 1968 Louis Alter was on the Board of Review and chairman of the Nominating Committee of ASCAP. Twelve of his best-known love songs were recorded in Italy by the Symphony Orchestra of the Rome Opera. His most important published song since the early 1960's was "Small Petroushka," lyrics by Johnny Mercer.

Leroy Anderson 1908-

For biographical sketch and list of earlier compositions see *Popular American Composers,* 1962.

———

In the 1960's Anderson became active in alumni affairs at Harvard University as trustee and first president of the Harvard Band Foundation, and as member of the Board of Overseers Visiting Committee to the Department of Music. In 1962 Anderson recorded an album for Decca containing six new instrumental compositions: *The Captains and the Kings, Clarinet Candy, The Golden Years, Home Stretch, Arietta,* and *Balladette.*

Anderson makes his home in Woodbury, Connecticut, where he and his wife, the former Eleanor Jane Pike (whom he married on October 31, 1942), raised four children.

1

Anka

Paul Anka 1941-

PAUL ANKA was born in Ottawa, Canada, on July 31, 1941, the oldest of three children. His father was a Syrian-born restaurant owner who served as vice-president of the Ottawa Chamber of Commerce. While attending grade school, Paul frequented theaters and nightclubs to study the style of outstanding popular singers. Revealing a gift for mimicry and impersonation, Paul often entertained his friends and neighbors with his performances. At ten he made his stage debut. Two years later, he and two high school classmates formed The Bobbysoxers, a singing trio which made local appearances. They soon were booked for theaters and clubs, for the Canada Exhibition in 1955, and at the Fairmount Club in Ottawa, where one evening Paul by himself won first prize in an amateur contest. All this time his father had objected to Paul's preoccupation with the stage. After attending one of his son's performances, however, he changed his mind and withdrew his opposition to Paul's stage ambitions.

Besides his interest in performing, Anka revealed from his childhood days a talent for writing songs, words as well as music. His melodies were often influenced by Syrian songs which he learned from his father. His first numbers were performed by The Bobbysoxers.

To further his career as composer, Anka used his savings to go to Los Angeles where his uncle was a nightclub entertainer and had connections with the motion picture and recording industries. In 1956, in Los Angeles, he succeeded in getting a small company to record one of his songs for the first time. The title of the song, "Blauwildesbestonstein," was the name of a South African city Anka had read about in a novel by John Buchan. This record sold only five thousand disks.

To earn money to return to Ottawa, Anka worked for a while as a movie usher. In Ottawa Anka continued to make

PAUL ANKA

Pietro Pascuttini

sporadic appearances as a singer, but his major activity was songwriting. One of his numbers, "Diana," was inspired by his love affair with an Ottawa girl three years his senior.

In 1957 Anka borrowed one hundred dollars and went to New York to try to market his songs. Despite his youth (he was not yet sixteen) he managed to penetrate the inner sanctum of ABC-Paramount Records—the office of Don Costa, Artists and Repertory head. "He leaped at the piano like it was a steak dinner and he hadn't eaten for months," Costa later recalled. Anka sang his numbers, including "Diana." Costa promptly offered him a long-term contract. Being under age, Anka had to bring his father from Ottawa to sign the contract.

Anka's first ABC-Paramount recording (and his first published song) was "Diana." Once released, it became a best seller and for thirteen consecutive weeks topped the best-seller lists. In a short period of time over three million disks were sold in America and six million more in the rest of the world. (Anka became the first Canadian ever to sell a million or more disks in a single year.) "Diana" had a lasting success. Within six years, three hundred and twenty recordings had been made in twenty-two countries. In all, some thirteen million copies have been sold, a figure few other recordings have achieved.

"You Are My Destiny," released in 1958, also achieved over a million-disk sale, as did its immediate successors the same year, "Lonely Boy" and "Put Your Head on My Shoulder." Thus Anka's first four records for ABC-Paramount were extraordinary hits.

His songs instantly made him a world personality, setting into motion his fruitful career as a singing performer. His first tour (1957-1958) brought him to Europe, Australia, and Japan where he was mobbed by his young admirers the moment he descended from his plane. In Japan two thousand youngsters defied a typhoon to stand in line all day to buy tickets for his concert. This was at a time when five of his songs appeared on a single Tokyo *Hit Parade* program. The American newspapers carried the story of his foreign triumphs. Upon returning to the United States in 1958, Anka received numerous offers to appear on television, in theaters, at concerts, and in the movies. His first motion picture (written to suit his special talents) was *Girls' Town*, released by MGM in 1959. This was followed by *The Private Lives of Adam and Eve* and *Look in Any Window*, both in 1960. Anka admits that all three were bad pictures but they were useful in providing him with an important showcase for his songs.

In 1958 and again in 1959 Anka embarked on other extensive foreign tours, creating great excitement wherever he appeared. "He has become a million-dollar bobbysox idol," commented Art Buchwald from Paris in his column. "On tour in North Africa . . . he had to have an escort of armed paratroopers to get from his hotel to the theater. Mr. Anka sang at the Monte Carlo Casino last week and went over big with what is usually considered a frigid audience." In Paris he outdrew Maurice Chevalier and Marlene Dietrich at the box office.

That Anka appealed to adults as well as bobbysoxers was proved in 1960 when he invaded the nightclub circuit, beginning in March with a booking at the Sahara in Las Vegas. In June he filled a highly successful three-week engagement at the famed Copacabana in New York. Extensive appearances in nightclubs throughout the United States, supplemented by guest appearances on major television programs, extended his adult public without losing his bobbysoxer following. By the end of 1960 Anka had his fifth straight million-copy disk in "Puppy Love." Up to and including 1960 he wrote other songs enjoying varying degrees of success, among them "It Doesn't Matter Any More," "Let the Bells Keep Ringing," "Crazy Love," "It's Time to Cry," "Adam and Eve," "Teddy," "Summer's Gone," "My Home Town," "Dance On, Little Girl," "It's Christmas Everywhere," and "A Broken Heart and a Pillow Filled with Tears."

The great success of his songs led Anka to organize two publishing houses, the Spanka and the Flanka, with some twenty overseas branches. To run the American firms, Anka's father gave up his own business interests in Canada. The whole Anka family came to the United States and, in 1960, settled in Tenafly, New Jersey.

When his contract with ABC-Paramount expired in 1961, Anka signed a long-term contract with RCA Victor and formed his own company (Camy Productions) to manufacture and package the records Victor would distribute. This venture proved so profitable that in 1963 Anka paid ABC-Paramount about a quarter of a million dollars to acquire all his earlier copyrights, master tapes, and reissue rights to avoid competition with his Victor releases. His recordings were now being made in five languages for international distribution; the first of these were made abroad during a world tour promoted by RCA Victor Records for Anka in 1962.

The year 1962 saw the release of Anka's first important motion picture, *The*

Longest Day, a Darryl Zanuck production about D-Day during World War II. Anka played the role of a Bronx boy serving with the American Rangers and also wrote the words and music of the title song which became popular that year. Other successful songs by Anka in 1961 and 1962 included "The Fool's Hall of Fame," "I Never Knew Your Name," "Love Me Warm and Tender," "A Steel Guitar and a Glass of Wine," "Tonight My Love, Tonight," and "Johnny's Song" which Anka had written in collaboration with Carson for the Johnny Carson nightly TV program.

A twelve-country tour in 1963 brought Anka behind the Iron Curtain for the first time. In Poland, where he went on an eight-day visit at the invitation of the government, he proved to be an extremely successful attraction. In 1964 he participated in the San Remo Festival in Italy. There he recorded "Ogni volti," which he sang in Italian, the first American to record a number in Italy surpassing a million disks in sales. Anka returned to the San Remo Festival in 1968 as one of two representatives (the other was Louis Armstrong) of the United States.

In 1964 Anka made his musical comedy debut in the United States by replacing Steve Lawrence in the Broadway musical *What Makes Sammy Run?* By then he had also starred in a motion picture short feature devoted to his career *(Lonely Boy).* This was voted the Canadian Film of the Year in 1963 and won seven international prizes.

Since 1963 Anka's principal songs have included "Did You Have a Happy Birthday?", "My Way," "Can't Get You Out of My Mind," "Life Goes On," and "Keeping One Foot in the Door." He wrote songs for artists other than himself. "My Way" (for which he wrote the English lyrics to a French song) was written for and introduced by Frank Sinatra, who made it a hit in the spring of 1969. (Forty other artists also recorded it.) "My Double Life" was written for and introduced by Buddy Greco. Comment-

ing on Anka's songwriting talent, Peter Reilly wrote in *Stereo Review* in 1970 that it "is highly professional and in a mature vein (which is all to the good, since there are so many mature performers in need of good material)."

By 1970 Anka had eighteen gold records to his credit and was believed to have sold over fifty million records in all. From royalties and personal appearances he draws about $1,500,000 a year. He makes his home in New York City with his wife, the former Anne de Zogheb, a fashion model and the daughter of Count and Countess Charles de Zogheb of Paris and Alexandria, Egypt. Anka and Anne first met in Puerto Rico in 1961 where Anka enjoyed such popularity that he had to be rescued from his fans by a helicopter when he was discovered shopping in a department store. They were married in the chapel of Orly Airport on February 16, 1963, and spent their honeymoon in Switzerland. They have two daughters: Alexandria, born in 1966, and Amanda, born in 1968. His active career as songwriter, recording artist, and singing star in nightclubs and concerts allows him too little time to spend with his family, and even less to indulge in favorite diversions such as swimming and skiing. Anka is an active member of the Syrian Orthodox Church. An anthology of his most famous songs, the *Paul Anka Song Book,* was issued in 1969.

In 1971 Anka ended his contractual agreement with RCA Victor to record for Epic on the Barnaby label distributed by CBS Records. Anka's first release for this new outfit featured two of his later songs: "You're Some Kind of a Friend" and "Why Are You Leaning on Me?"

ABOUT:

Roxon, L. *Rock Encyclopedia.*
Coronet, May 1961; Current Biography, February 1964; Life, August 29, 1960.

Harry Archer 1888-1960

See *Popular American Composers,* 1962.

Harold Arlen 1905-

For biographical sketch and list of earlier songs see *Popular American Composers,* 1962.

———

Arlen wrote the music to E. Y. Harburg's lyrics for the songs Judy Garland and Robert Goulet performed on the soundtrack of the full-length animated cartoon *Gay Purr-ee,* released by Warner Brothers in 1962. They were "Paris Is a Lonely Town," "Take My Hand, Paree," "Musette," and "Little Drops of Rain." In 1963 Judy Garland once again presented an Arlen-Harburg number in motion pictures when she sang the title number of *I Could Go On Singing.* Arlen's "So Long, Big Time" (lyrics by Dory Langdon) was introduced by Tony Bennett in *Twentieth Century,* a 1964 TV documentary honoring Arlen.

After Arlen married the actress Anya Tarandain Harrison in New Jersey on January 8, 1937, they occupied a house on Lookout Mountain Road in Laurel Canyon, Beverly Hills, California. Two decades later the Arlens transferred their permanent residence to a duplex apartment in the East Fifties in New York City where they now live and where Arlen pursues his hobbies, reading and painting.

Felix Arndt 1889-1918

See *Popular American Composers, 1962.*

Burt Bacharach 1928-

THOUGH he has never identified himself with rock 'n' roll or country and western music, Burt Bacharach is one of the most successful, distinguished, and original songwriters to appear on the American music scene in many years. He was born in Kansas City, Missouri, on May 12, 1928. His father, Bert Bacharach, was a clothing buyer for a department store; his mother, a painter.

BURT BACHARACH

The family moved to New York City when Burt was two years old. His father joined the staff of *Collier's,* then became a columnist for the *Journal-American* and later, in the 1950's, published two books, *Book for Men* and *Right Dress.* After the move, Burt's mother gave up art to devote herself to her family. Burt grew up in the Forest Hills section of Queens where he attended public schools. Since he revealed unmistakable signs of musical talent, his parents encouraged him to play an instrument. He studied on a borrowed cello, then tried playing the drums, and finally decided to concentrate on the piano. His parents, who hoped he would someday become a serious composer, saw to it that he pursued music study assiduously. "My folks kept my interest in music going when I hated it," he revealed to Rex Reed in the New York *Times.* "It was very lonely practicing the piano while my friends were out playing touch football and I was inside playing Tchaikovsky's 'None But the Lonely Heart.' Also, I was Jewish and all my friends were Catholics. They always got to do things together, like going to midnight Mass. I couldn't go. . . . So, to be the life of the party, I played piano in a Friday night dance band and

5

suddenly I was with a real group of musicians, practicing together, meeting people. Music made me belong." His favorites were Dizzy Gillespie and Harry James.

Immediately following World War II, he was chosen to tour Army hospitals playing boogie-woogie. One summer later he formed a quintet which found a job playing in a hotel in the Catskill Mountains in New York. "We were like prisoners," he recalls. "One morning we woke up to fire engines. The hotel had burned down. We cheered."

Bacharach received a comprehensive training calculated to develop him for a career not in popular but in serious music. He studied at the Mannes School of Music in New York; during the summers at the Berkshire Music Center at Tanglewood, in Lenox, Massachusetts; with Darius Milhaud at the Music Academy of the West in Santa Barbara, California (on a scholarship) and later at McGill University in Montreal. Besides Milhaud, his most important teachers included Bohuslav Martinu and Henry Cowell. In spite of this background, he still preferred popular music. He explained: "I started seeing the dedication, the way serious composers had to teach school to live, waiting for grants to be able to eat, the poor money they made. I didn't dig it."

Between 1950 and 1952 he served in the armed forces. Assigned to play the piano at the officers' club at Governors Island and to give concerts at Fort Dix, he had to rely on improvisations and medleys of Broadway tunes for his programs, since he had not yet acquired a basic popular repertory. Frequently he made up tunes spontaneously, and when asked what they were he would reply "an unpublished work by Debussy." He kept this up, living off the base, until he was dispatched to Germany where he did arrangements for a German dance band.

After his discharge from the Army, Bacharach was hired by the singer Vic Damone as accompanist. This job did not last long, but he found employment as pianist with other singers including Imogene Coca, the Ames Brothers, Paula Stewart, and Polly Bergen. With Polly Bergen he worked on a ship that made a nightly cruise between Washington and Baltimore. "He was a wonderful accompanist," she recalls. "Why, he knew when I was going to breathe before I did." Paula Stewart became Bacharach's first wife, but they remained married only three years.

He decided to become a composer of popular tunes while he was performing in Las Vegas with the Ames Brothers. The popular songs he played for them were, he thought, so awful that he was convinced he could do much better. "So," as he said to his interviewer, "I told myself I should quit, go back to New York and write a hit." He hired an office in the Brill Building in New York where he worked every day for ten months writing song after song. He could not get a single one published. To support himself he played the piano during the evenings for Joel Grey, Georgia Gibbs, and Steve Lawrence. Finally, one of his songs was recorded by Patti Page. "It was awful," he says. "I'd rather forget it." Two other songs, however, were more to his satisfaction. One was "The Story of My Life," introduced by Marty Robbins in a Columbia recording, and the other was "Magic Moments," sung by Perry Como for Victor. Both were released in 1957, and both had lyrics by Hal David with whom he would henceforth work so successfully. In 1958 came "Hot Spell," inspired by the motion picture of the same name, and "The Blob," heard in the movie with that title.

In 1958 he worked as arranger and conductor for Marlene Dietrich during her personal appearances in America and Europe. He remained with Miss Dietrich for three years. "She's the most generous and giving woman I know," he says. When Miss Dietrich first heard Bacharach's "Warm and Tender" she immediately telephoned Frank Sinatra to urge him to use it. When he turned it down she prophesied: "Some day you'll be asking him to write songs for you." "He used to tell me to relax and sit back and let the notes come," Miss Dietrich has said of Bacharach. "When you know he is looking after you you can sit back. . . . He's my teacher, he's my critic, he's my accompanist, he's my arranger, he's my conductor." Miss Dietrich continued to call on Bacharach to help rehearse the musicians and sometimes conduct her concert appearances even after the songwriter became famous, and Bacharach usually responded. He worked for Miss Dietrich in her performances in Copenhagen and London; in 1968 she postponed her Broadway concert debut until Bacharach was free of contractual commitments in Hollywood. "Marlene taught me a lot about not settling for less," Bacharach told Reed. "I just watched her—what she went after, what she's got. The time I spent with her is worth ten song hits."

Far more strongly identified with Bacharach's career is another singer, Dionne Warwicke. When he first heard her in 1962 she was an unknown background singer who had majored in music at the Hartt College of Music at the University of Hartford in Connecticut. Hearing her sing for the first time Bacharach felt, as he said, "she just shone just as she shines now." Bacharach had the young unknown singer record his "Don't Make Me Over," released in 1962. Since then Dionne Warwicke has recorded all the songs Bacharach and Hal David wrote (over two hundred), and they have sold over fifteen million disks. Among her Bacharach record successes are "I Just Don't Know What To Do with Myself," "What the World Needs Now Is Love," "Please Make Him Love Me," "Anyone Who Had a Heart," "Close to You," "The Girl's in Love," "What Do You Get When You Fall in Love?", "Knowing When to Leave," "Walk On By," "Any Old Time of Day," "A Message to Michael," "The Look of Love," "This Guy's in Love with You,"

"Let Me Go to Him," "Do You Know the Way to San Jose?", "Only Love Can Break a Heart," and "Paper Maché."

The years 1962 and 1963 were highly productive for Bacharach. Two motion pictures used his title songs: *Forever My Love* and *Wonderful to Be Young.* "The Man Who Shot Liberty Valance" was a song inspired by the motion picture of that name. Bacharach was now emerging as a songwriter with a gift for highly personalized melodies—not the kind of tune easily remembered and readily whistled but melodies developed along highly original and unconventional lines, filled with interesting rhythmic patterns and changing meters. In such a fresh, invigorating style was the hit song "Wives and Lovers" ("Hey, Little Girl"), from the motion picture of the same name, which became a best seller in Jack Jones's recording in 1963. It received an Emmy as the "best solo male vocal performance." Bacharach's output in 1963 included "Who's Been Sleeping in My Bed?", suggested by the movie of that title released in 1964, "Wishin' and Hopin'," "Twenty-four Hours from Tulsa," "Blue on Blue," "Reach Out for Me," and "Anonymous Phone Call." In 1964 Doris Day introduced the title song of the motion picture *Send Me No Flowers.* The same year saw the birth of several other individually styled songs, including "There's Always Something There to Remind Me," "A Lifetime of Loneliness," "Any Old Time of Day," "Trains, Boats and Planes," and "You'll Never Get to Heaven," among others.

Bacharach married Angie Dickinson, the motion picture star, in 1965. They settled in a rented house in Beverly Hills where a daughter, Nikki, was born to them in 1966. "The baby was born three months premature and weighed only a pound and ten ounces," Bacharach told Rex Reed. "They gave her half of one percent chance to live through the first night. Angie was a very sick girl, with an infection through her whole body. I almost lost both of them, but they made it, and now that gratefulness, that vivid remembrance, not impaired by the passing of time, is so strong that I will never take what I've got for granted. I'm very sentimental about my family. Looking at them, I see things that are much more important than writing hit songs."

Nevertheless, the hit songs kept coming, most of them introduced in motion pictures. The year 1965 brought the title number of the first motion picture for which Bacharach wrote a complete score—*What's New, Pussycat?*", which included the title song and "My Little Red Book." In 1966 Trini Lopez introduced the title song of *Made in Paris* on its soundtrack. For the title song of *Alfie* (which was eventually recorded by more than one hundred performers) Bacharach received a nomination for an Academy Award in 1967; this was another movie for which he was responsible for the complete score. He was again nominated for an Academy Award in 1968 for the bossa nova "The Look of Love" from *Casino Royale*. In 1969, however, he captured not one but two Academy Awards for the motion picture *Butch Cassidy and the Sundance Kid*: for the scoring, and for the song "Raindrops Keep Fallin' on My Head." The scoring also won a Grammy award. "Raindrops Keep Fallin' on My Head" sold over three million records in B. J. Thomas's rendition, and over one million copies of sheet music.

Among other Bacharach hit songs are "Odds and Ends" recorded by Johnny Mathis, "She's Gone Away," "Pacific Coast Highway," "A House Is Not a Home," "Everybody's Gone Out Of Town," "Walk On By," "I Just Don't Know What to Do with Myself," "Make It Easy on Yourself," "Don't Go Breaking My Heart," "They Don't Give Medals," "Here I Am," "Are You There," "The Windows of the World," and "I Say a Little Prayer." "And the People with Her," a five-minute orchestral ballad, was recorded in 1971 in the album *Burt Bacharach*.

Commenting on a typical Bacharach hit song, Hubert Saal wrote in *Newsweek* that "it pulsates restlessly, charges up and down the scale recklessly, rouses itself from a dying fall into an atomic explosion. The dynamics of 'Walk On By' range from a double pianissimo to a triple forte." Mr. Saal then adds: "It's a lopsided kind of music, full of surprises which keep it fresh and vital and keep the listener off balance. More than anything, it's alive, with an inner tension, a restrained energy that is intensely dramatic. Even a cantering song . . . seethes with tension; each downbeat is restrained violence and the loping meter is like the gait of a horse ready to gather its bulging muscles and surge over some high fence."

Bacharach made his Broadway debut on December 1, 1968, with *Promises, Promises*. This is the often brilliant, always amusing musical comedy adaptation by Neil Simon of the screen comedy *The Apartment*. The musical had a good deal to commend it, and it became a box office success. Not the least of its assets was Bacharach's score which included a resounding hit number in "I'll Never Fall in Love Again," whose success is all the more remarkable in that it depends for its appeal not on an infectious melody but upon its strong, insistent beat, its multiple time values, and other subtleties. Other strong numbers in the show were "Whoever You Are, I Love You" and "Where Can You Take a Girl?" But the outstanding characteristics of Bacharach's score were the quality and the dynamism of its sound, something quite new for Broadway. Bacharach explained: "I tried to get the right musicians, who could play my kind of pop music, instead of the usual pit orchestra. I went for younger guys. I put in an electronic booth to control the choral voices I used with the music. I inserted fiberglass panels to separate the sound from mike to mike and tried to achieve the same conditions you get in a recording session without the isolated sound of music coming through speakers. It's a very complicated electronic system with echo chambers and equalizers and technical equipment. . . . If we knocked down a few doors with my rhythms and new sounds in the show, *great*. Show music has to move on."

Martin Gottfried said of Bacharach's first Broadway score: "A real breakthrough for Broadway. . . . The whole archaic system of show-biz has been shattered. Bacharach has proved that modern music can be put live in the theater." The New York critics selected Bacharach as the best composer of the Broadway season and Hal David as the best lyricist. The original-cast recording was awarded a Grammy.

In 1969 Bacharach and his father were collectively honored as Man of the Year at the March of Dimes dinner in New York City. During the same year Bacharach was the subject of a TV documentary telecast coast to coast. Since then he has frequently starred on his own television specials, one of which—*The Sound of Bacharach* sponsored by Kraft Music Hall on NBC—received an Emmy award in 1970. Another Bacharach special received an Emmy in 1971. In March of 1970 Bacharach made his nightclub debut at Harrah's in Tahoe, with a sixty-minute production devoted exclusively to his songs. He appeared as commentator, orchestral arranger, conductor, and pianist-singer as well as composer. "A full house . . . assured the tunesmith he's writing (and riding) on a responsive line," reported the *Variety* critic, adding: "Palmed endorsements were coincident with opening bars of all . . . offerings—from his initial 'Do You Know the Way to San Jose?' to the bravo'd exit to 'What the World Needs Now Is Love.' " Now a sex symbol as well as an ace performer and composer, Bacharach sold out five performances at the Westbury Music Fair in New York in May, and eight performances in one week at the Greek Theater in Los Angeles in July; at the latter, he broke all box office records in the eighteen-year history of that auditorium.

In describing Bacharach's conducting, Hubert Saal says "he has a calisthenically emotional style . . . that involves doing simultaneous knee bends at the piano, swiveling to fire musical directions at the different sections of the band, using his hands like karate choppers, generating an excitement among the musicians and . . . the audience."

Compounding success upon success, Bacharach—above and beyond his triumphs on television, in public concerts, and in writing for the movies—had no less than three albums of his songs on the best-seller lists in 1970: *Make It Easy on Yourself, Reach Out,* and *Butch Cassidy and the Sundance Kid.* In making his own recordings, he scrupulously supervises the doctoring of all tapes, does his own orchestrations, and conducts the orchestra.

According to *Newsweek* in its cover story "The Music Man 1970," Bacharach is earning a fortune not only from his music but from other business endeavors. He receives on the average of $35,000 a week for his concert appearances; half the publishing rights to his movie scores and songs; 8 percent of the income on his own recordings for A & M Records, and about a million and a half dollars a year from Scepter Records for releases of his songs performed by Dionne Warwicke and B. J. Thomas; 2 percent of the gross of *Promises, Promises;* and additional royalties or income from five other companies in the United States and Europe. He owns a publishing house valued at two million dollars, two restaurants, a car-washing service in New Jersey, real estate in Georgia, and a herd of five hundred cattle.

Outside his career and his family his main interest is his racing stable comprising at least six horses (one of which cost him $40,000). The very first horse he bought, Battle Royal, won its first race—an event Bacharach looks back upon as one of the greatest thrills he has known. He goes to the racetrack as often as his many activities allow (which he regrets is not often enough).

Though his home is in Beverly Hills, he retains his old bachelor apartment on East Sixty-first Street in New York. This flat, which he has occupied for years, is usually in a state of total disorder. It is his hideout when he must be in New York while his wife and daughter are in California; when they come to New York to join him they occupy a hotel suite.

About his songwriting he has said: "I can write songs anywhere. If Angie is making a picture in Arizona, I can write in the hotel room. . . . But I can't write anything at the piano. I write everything in my head and then put it down on paper." Since he began working with his principal lyricist, Hal David, in 1957, he has conformed to no set method of operation. Sometimes David gets an idea for a lyric from a melodic or rhythmic pattern Bacharach plays for him. Sometimes Bacharach gets his theme from a suggestion by his collaborator. They have, from the very beginning, worked most harmoniously, with little of the wear and tear on the nerves and none of the bitter altercations that so often characterize such collaborations. "The key to Hal," Bacharach told Saal, "is his flexibility. He's a terribly nice guy. When he writes 'What the world needs now is love, sweet love,' he believes it. He's kind and gentle, which is important when you have to stay in a room with him all day." Their sole problem is that Hal David smokes continually and Bacharach is annoyed by the odor. But Bacharach has become tolerant because once when David gave up smoking for three months his personality changed for the worse; Bacharach was delighted when his partner reverted to his vice. Says Hal David about his working sessions with Bacharach: "The air is always clear—except for my smoking."

The Bacharach and David Song Book, containing thirty-seven Bacharach hit songs, was published in 1970.

ABOUT:

Ascap Today, August 1970; Current Biography, October 1970; New York Times, December 15, 1968; Newsweek, June 22, 1970.

Ernest R. Ball 1878-1927

See *Popular American Composers,* 1962.

Irving Berlin 1888-

For biographical sketch and list of earlier songs see *Popular American Composers,* 1962.

National and international politics, which had been the theme of Berlin's musical comedy *Call Me Madam* (1950) served once again for his Broadway musical, *Mr. President,* in 1962. The family life in the White House of a fictional American President at the close of his Administration, his complications with the Soviet Union when he insists upon visiting that country after his invitation has been revoked, the return of the President and his family to the obscurity of non-political life following the election of a new President, and his final decision to return to the political scene—all this makes up the serviceable text of the show in which Robert Ryan played the President and Nanette Fabray his wife. Two songs from Berlin's score are particularly notable: "Empty Pockets Filled with Love" and "Meat and Potatoes"; of secondary interest are "Pigtails and Freckles" and "Is He the Only Man in the World?"

In 1966 Berlin told an interviewer: "It's nice to hear compliments about the many standards I've written over the years, but I can also hear that little bird behind me chirping, 'So what have you done lately?' " Berlin's answer could have been that he had written a new song hit "An Old-Fashioned Wedding," which brought down the house at every performance of *Annie Get Your Gun* in its outstanding revival at the New York State Theater of the Lincoln Center for the Performing Arts on May 31, 1966; that he produced three new songs for *Call Me Madam* when that musical became a two-hour special on television in 1968; that he came up with a new song, "I Used to Play

It by Ear," which Robert Goulet introduced on the Ed Sullivan program honoring Berlin on his eightieth birthday on May 5, 1968. That program, devoted exclusively to Berlin's songs, was the first to which Ed Sullivan devoted an hour and a half, instead of the usual hour. It began with a taped message from President Johnson and ended with Berlin himself on the stage singing "God Bless America." Bob Hope paid a special tribute to Berlin, and the principal performers, besides Hope and Goulet, included Ethel Merman, The Supremes, and Fred Waring and his Pennsylvanians.

Other tributes helped Berlin celebrate his eightieth birthday. The television program "Hollywood Palace" did a Berlin program three weeks before Ed Sullivan's; six days after the Ed Sullivan show, a radio station in Dublin, Ireland, offered an Irving Berlin program. At the Radio City Music Hall in New York on May 1, Leon Leonidoff produced the stage presentation, "Words and Music by Irving Berlin."

Elmer Bernstein 1922-

SINCE the middle 1950's, Elmer Bernstein has been a prolific and successful composer of background music for motion pictures. From some of these scores, passages were lifted and transformed into popular songs with superimposed lyrics. From other scores came the words and music of title numbers, a few of which achieved substantial success.

Bernstein was trained for a career in serious music. Born in New York City on April 14, 1922, he attended the Walden School and New York University. He began his musical training in early boyhood, later specializing in the piano at the Juilliard School of Music, and studying composition with Roger Sessions. On December 21, 1946, Bernstein married Pearl Glasman with whom he had two sons. Also in 1946, he made his debut as concert pianist, a career he pursued for the

ELMER BERNSTEIN

next few years with recitals in various American cities. During this time he wrote some serious music which did not receive important concert performances.

Bernstein made the transition from serious to popular music in 1949 by writing music for radio programs produced by the United Nations. A year later Columbia Pictures put him under contract to write for the movies. The next two decades and more saw him create scores for numerous successful motion pictures. In these scores he made a conscious effort to compose music basic to the dramatic sequences on the screen. Few composers have proved more skillful in projecting atmosphere, building up suspense, stressing emotion, and intensifying drama through music.

His first important assignment after a period of valuable apprenticeship, was the score for *The Man with the Golden Arm* (1955), starring Frank Sinatra, which brought the composer a nomination for an Academy Award. Some years later a theme was lifted from this music to become the popular song "Molly-O" (lyrics by Sylvia Fine). Before the 1950's ended, Bernstein had written the background music for the following major films: *The Ten Commandments,* directed

11

by Cecil B. De Mille (1956); *The Sweet Smell of Success,* starring Burt Lancaster (1957); *Desire Under the Elms,* with Sophia Loren (1958); *God's Little Acre* (1958); and *Kings Go Forth* and *Some Came Running,* both starring Frank Sinatra in 1958.

Between 1960 and 1962 Bernstein was again nominated for Academy Awards for scores to *The Magnificent Seven, Summer and Smoke,* and *Walk on the Wild Side.* The principal theme in *Summer and Smoke* became popular as an instrumental composition; so did the major musical themes of scores from two other motion pictures released during these two years, *The Rat Race* and *From the Terrace.* Themes from the score of *Walk on the Wild Side,* with lyrics by Mack David, received successful recordings as popular songs entitled "Walk on the Wild Side" and "Somewhere in the Used to Be." In addition, Sammy Cahn provided lyrics to a melody from Bernstein's score for *By Love Possessed;* Mack David, for themes from the score to *The Girl from Tamiko* and for a melody from *The Bird Man of Alcatraz.* This one, a number called "The Bird Man," was successfully recorded in 1962 by the Highwaymen for United Artists.

Since 1962 Bernstein has written not only background music but often the melodies for songs for major screen productions. Among these motion pictures are *To Kill a Mockingbird* starring Gregory Peck, winner of the Golden Globe Award of the Foreign Press Association; *Hud,* with Paul Newman; *Love with the Proper Stranger,* with Steve McQueen and Natalie Wood; *The Great Escape,* with Steve McQueen; *The Carpetbaggers; The World of Henry Orient,* with Peter Sellers; *Baby, the Rain Must Fall,* with Steve McQueen and Lee Remick; *The Sons of Katie Elder,* with John Wayne; *The Hallelujah Trail; Ship of Fools; The Silencers,* with Dean Martin; *Hawaii,* with Julie Andrews; *Thoroughly Modern Millie,* with Julie Andrews; *Where's Jack?; True Grit; The Liberation of L. B. Jones; Cannon for Cordoba; Doctors' Wives; A Walk in the Spring Rain; Big Jake,* starring John Wayne; and *See No Evil.*

For his score to *Thoroughly Modern Millie,* Bernstein received the Academy Award in 1968. Among the noteworthy songs to emerge from some of the productions listed above were the title numbers of *By Love Possessed* (Sammy Cahn); *To Kill a Mockingbird* (Mack David), introduced in a recording by Vincent Edwards; *Love with the Proper Stranger* (Johnny Mercer), popularized by Jack Jones, who had sung it on the soundtrack of the motion picture and then for a best-selling recording; *Baby, the Rain Must Fall* (Ernie Sheldon), introduced in the motion picture by the We Three, but made successful in 1965 by Glenn Yarbrough. In *Hawaii,* Julie Andrews introduced "My Wishing Doll" (Mack David).

In 1964 Bernstein was awarded an Emmy for his background music to the television documentary *The Making of a President.*

Bernstein's debut as a composer for the Broadway musical theater came in 1967 with *How Now, Dow Jones,* lyrics by Carolyn Leigh. This was a comedy about Wall Street and what happens when the "Dow Jones girl," motivated by her boyfriend's promise to marry her when the Dow Jones average hits a certain high, throws the financial world into a spin with a false report that its average reached the thousand mark. The musical failed, but one of Bernstein's songs was a winner: "Step to the Rear" (perhaps better known as "Let a Winner Lead the Way"). This number became involved in the presidential campaign of 1968. Publicized as Hubert Humphrey's campaign song (with lyrics altered for this purpose by Humphrey's daughter, Mrs. Solomonson), it had to be dropped by the Democratic party when the discovery was made that the necessary permission rights had not been properly cleared with the authors.

Bernstein was elected president of the Young Musicians Fund in 1961. On April 7, 1970, he served as a musical director of the forty-second annual presentation of awards by the Academy of Motion Picture Arts and Sciences in which his title song for *True Grit* (lyrics by Don Black) had been one of the nominations. This song received the ASCAP Award on October 16, 1969, in Nashville, Tennessee, as one of the best country records of the year.

In 1970 Bernstein became vice-president of the Academy of Motion Picture Arts and Sciences and president of the Composers and Lyricists Guild of America.

ABOUT:
ASCAP Biographical Dictionary (1966).

Leonard Bernstein 1918-

For biographical sketch and list of earlier songs see *Popular American Composers,* 1962.

———

The motion picture adaptation of the stage musical *West Side Story* (1957), released in 1961, became an extraordinary box office attraction the world over. It received ten Academy Awards, including that of the best picture of the year. As a stage production it entered the regular opera repertory of the Volksoper in Vienna in 1969 after having been successfully revived in New York at the Lincoln Center for the Performing Arts a year earlier.

Bernstein's first musical, *On the Town* (1944)—which subsequently received two Off-Broadway revivals—was produced in London in 1963, and opened on Broadway in the fall of 1971. *Candide,* a failure in 1956, was revived in San Francisco in 1971 before an announced Broadway run.

When Bernstein resigned as music director of the New York Philharmonic Orchestra in 1969, he was given a life appointment as "laureate conductor" with the opportunity to appear as guest conductor of that organization whenever he wished. He left this post (which he had held, with such distinction, longer than any other previous music director) to devote more time to composing and to make guest appearances with orchestras and opera companies in America and Europe.

Bernstein has published two books since *The Joy of Music* (1954): *The Infinite Variety of Music* (1966) and *Leonard Bernstein's Children's Concerts* (1970).

William Billings 1746-1800

See *Popular American Composers,* 1962.

James A. Bland 1854-1911

See *Popular American Composers,* 1962.

Jerry Bock 1928-

For biographical sketch and list of earlier songs see *Popular American Composers,* 1962.

———

"Never Too Late" was an instrumental cha-cha which Bock wrote for the nonmusical Broadway play *Never Too Late* (1962). During the next two years individual numbers by Bock (lyrics by Sheldon Harnick) included "Worlds Apart," introduced in a marionette play produced by Cora Baird, and "Popsickles in Paris," heard in *To Broadway with Love,* a musical written for and produced at the New York World's Fair in 1964.

Meanwhile, in 1963, with Harnick, Bock supplied the songs for the Broadway musical *She Loves Me,* a warmhearted and tender musical adapted from the motion picture *The Little Shop Around the Corner.* Though hardly a success (301 performances), it will probably be remembered for its best songs, including "Dear Friend," "Days Gone By," and the title number—a score good enough to bring Bock the designation of the composer of the year by the New York Critics poll.

Fiddler on the Roof (with lyrics by Harnick), which opened in the fall of 1964, was—to use a word from the review in *Variety*—a "blockbuster." Based on stories by Sholem Aleichem (as adapted by Joseph Stein) about old-world Jews and their exotic rituals and ways of life, *Fiddler on the Roof* became one of the greatest successes in the history of the Broadway theater, and one of the best musicals of the twentieth century. How much of a "blockbuster" it really would be, not even the critic of *Variety* (or anybody else including those involved in the production) could have dared to guess. It became the longest-running musical in Broadway history on July 21, 1971, when it presented its 2,845th performance (playing almost always to sold-out houses). It received nine Tony awards, including that of the best musical of the season, and the New York Drama Critics Award. By 1971 the receipts at the box office in New York went well beyond twenty million dollars. Over a million dollars' worth of the original-cast recording was sold and the motion picture rights brought in another two million dollars. Performances by touring companies throughout the United States contributed still another fifteen million dollars. In addition, income poured in from productions in foreign capitals from Tokyo to Tel Aviv, from Sydney to Copenhagen, from Istanbul to Iceland. In 1970 it even entered the repertory of a world-famous opera house—the Komische Oper in East Berlin. Wherever it was given it was a triumph because (as Howard Taubman reported in the New York *Times* after the Broadway opening) it was filled "with laughter and tenderness. It catches the essence of a moment in history with sentiment and radiance. Compounded of the familiar materials of the musical theater . . . it combines and transcends

them to arrive at an integrated achievement of uncommon quality."

Though Jerry Bock's music is made up essentially of characteristic Broadway tunes, some had intervallic structures to provide a Jewish flavoring, making them particularly suitable for a Russian-Jewish background and characters. One number, "Sunrise, Sunset" became a hit. But others were hardly less memorable, including "If I Were a Rich Man," "To Life," "Tradition," and "Matchmaker, Matchmaker." Said Mr. Taubman: "The score . . . moves the story along, enriching the mood and intensifying the emotions." The New York Critics poll once again selected Bock as the composer of the year. Noteworthy, too, in this remarkable production were the direction and choreography of Jerome Robbins.

Fiddler on the Roof was followed by *Generation* (1965) in which Bock's lyricist was not Harnick but William Goodman; the show was a failure. Of far greater interest was *The Apple Tree* (1966), an unusual Off-Broadway production in which Harnick once again served as Bock's lyricist. *The Apple Tree* was made up of three one-act musicals, based on three different stories (by Mark Twain, Frank R. Stockton, and Jules Feiffer). Each segment concerned itself with Woman: with Eve in the Garden of Eden; with Princess Barbara, a character in a semibarbaric kingdom in the distant past; and with a modern motion-picture sex symbol. To a text filled with mockery and satire, Bock contributed a delightful score whose best numbers were "Forbidden Love" (a parody on songs praising far-off lands), "I've Got What You Want" (a travesty on sexy songs), and "What Makes Me Love Him."

On October 18, 1970, a new Bock-Harnick musical opened on Broadway. It was *The Rothschilds,* based on Frederick Morton's best-selling history tracing the House of Rothschild from its founding in 1717 by Mayer Rothschild through 1818 when it had become Eu-

14

rope's most powerful banking institution, run by Mayer's five sons. *The Rothschilds,* as a text, had Jewish appeal, and some of Bock's songs had a Jewish personality—for example, "Tossed a Coin" in which the oldest of the Rothschilds describes his origins as a peddler in Frankfurt. "Mr. Bock's music," said Clive Barnes in the New York *Times,* "makes a neat nod in the direction of the eighteenth century, but blends period pastiche with a gentler, more cultivated version of those Jewish folk melodies that were so successful in *Fiddler on the Roof.* The fiddle has become a violin, but it still sounds pretty sweet." However, there is in this music far less emphasis on Jewish-sounding melodies than in *Fiddler on the Roof.* As Bock explained, most of his music is "in the classic tradition of eighteenth and nineteenth century Európean music." In the first act, a baroque trumpet is used in the orchestration to recreate an eighteenth century musical sound, while brass instruments are stressed in the second act to speak musically for the nineteenth century. Individual numbers do not stand out prominently, though "I'm in Love," "One Room," and "In My Own Lifetime" are pleasant. Bock's main interest lay in blending his music with the text. This score as a whole has professional polish and, together with Michael Kidd's staging, made an important contribution to a production which Clive Barnes said has wit, moral force, and style.

Carrie Jacobs Bond 1862-1946

See *Popular American Composers,* 1962.

David Braham 1838-1905

See *Popular American Composers,* 1962.

Shelton Brooks 1886-

See *Popular American Composers,* 1962.

Nacio Herb Brown 1896-1964

For biographical sketch and list of songs see *Popular American Composers,* 1962.

———

After an illness of eighteen months, Nacio Herb Brown died of cancer in San Francisco, California, on September 28, 1964.

Boudleaux Bryant 1920-

WHILE the husband-and-wife songwriting team of Boudleaux and Felice Bryant are best known for their country and western music, they have also produced numerous songs in other styles, including traditional "pop" numbers, ballads, novelty songs, and instrumental pieces. Over seven hundred of their songs have been recorded, with a total sale of close to one hundred million disks.

Boudleaux Bryant was born in Shellman, Georgia, on February 13, 1920. While he was an infant, his family moved to Moultrie, Georgia, where Boudleaux began to study the violin at the age of five. He continued these lessons for thirteen years, hoping to become a concert performer. He never did become a virtuoso, but in 1938 he played in various orchestras including the Atlanta Philharmonic.

The transition to popular music came in 1939. In a violin maker's shop he met a representative of radio station WSB, Atlanta, who was then in need of a violinist for a radio ensemble specializing in country music. Bryant asked for and received the job. For the next decade he played with various popular music groups in clubs and hotels in different parts of the country, as well as on the radio—usually in small "combos" devoted to country-western music and jazz.

In 1945 Boudleaux Bryant was performing at The Schroeder Hotel, Milwaukee, where the elevator operator was Felice Scaduto. She was born in Mil-

BOUDLEAUX BRYANT

waukee, Wisconsin, on August 7, 1925, and from childhood on had been trained as a singer. The two began dating; before 1945 ended they were married. Their honeymoon was spent at the Gibson Hotel in Cincinnati where Boudleaux was booked for an engagement of several months.

Up to this time, Boudleaux had been writing songs mostly as a hobby, achieving no public recognition, though a few were recorded by Texas "swing" bands. After marrying Felice, Boudleaux began to take songwriting more seriously. In this, he and his wife sometimes collaborated, working together on both words and music to become in time the most successful husband-and-wife songwriting combination in popular music.

But that success took time in coming. The Bryants completed some eighty numbers without getting a single one published or recorded. Finally, through the influence of Rome Johnson, then affiliated with Acuff-Rose Publishing Company in Nashville, Tennessee, the Bryants gained access to Fred Rose who accepted several Bryant numbers for publication. One was "Country Boy," which Jimmie Dickens recorded and which sold over 350,000 disks.

In 1950 the Bryants moved to Nashville where they worked as representatives for Tannen Music, a New York publisher. During their four years in this post they wrote "Have a Good Time" in 1952 which both Tony Bennett and Billy Eckstine recorded and which was successfully revived in 1962 by Sue Thompson. "Just Wait 'Til I Get You Alone" was the Bryants' most successful effort in 1953. On his own, Boudleaux Bryant wrote the words and music of "Hey Joe" in 1953, and "Back Up, Buddy" and "I've Been Thinking" in 1954, the last a best seller in Eddy Arnold's recording.

The Bryants left Tannen in 1954 to form Showcase Music, their own publishing venture. Two years later they signed a ten-year contract as writers with Acuff-Rose. When this contract was terminated, the Bryants organized a new firm to publish their songs—Bryant Publications in Hendersonville, a suburb of Nashville.

It was through some of their songs (written either by both Bryants or by Boudleaux alone) that the young singing duo, the Everly Brothers, first became famous in the 1950's. Among the numbers that helped bring them their success were "Bye Bye Love," "Wake Up Little Susie," "All I Have to Do Is Dream," "Bird Dog," "Devoted to You," "Problems," "Poor Jenny," and "Take a Message to Mary"—the last three being the only ones in which Boudleaux collaborated with his wife. Other Bryant hit songs in the 1950's were recorded by various other artists: Frankie Laine ("Hawk-Eye"); Eddy Arnold ("The Richest Man in the World"); Jim Reeves ("Blue Doll"). All these were solo efforts by Boudleaux. Some of the recordings mentioned above sold over a million disks each, notably, "Bye Bye Love," "All I Have to Do Is Dream," "Wake Up Little Susie," and "Bird Dog."

Another performer who owed some of his biggest recordings hits in the 1950's to Bryant's songs was Carl Smith. His best sellers were "It's a Lovely, Lovely

World," "Our Honeymoon," "This Orchid Means Goodbye" (in which Boudleaux collaborated with Carl Smith), and "Back Up, Buddy." Smith did well also with Bryant songs previously recorded by others—particularly with "Hey Joe" and "Just Wait 'Til I Get You Alone."

In the 1960's, Boudleaux Bryant branched out into instrumental music with *Mexico*. Besides achieving hit status in America it sold over a million records in West Germany, and within a few years accumulated a sale of well over six million disks in various recordings, including one by Herb Alpert's Tijuana Brass. More ambitious in structure and instrumentation was *Polynesian Suite*, a tonal portrait of the South Sea Islands that took Bryant six months to write.

Songwriting, of course, was not neglected; and the hits kept coming. With Skeeter Davis, Boudleaux contributed the lyrics to "My Last Date" (music by Floyd Cramer). Without a collaborator Bryant wrote "Let's Think About Living," and with his wife, "Baltimore" and "I Love to Dance with Annie."

In 1970 "Country Gentleman" (which Boudleaux Bryant wrote with Chet Atkins) received a Grammy as the best instrumental recording of country music (performed by the Nashville Brass). In the same year, BMI selected Bryant's "All I Have to Do Is Dream" and "Raining in My Heart" for special awards as among the most popular country music in the repertory.

ABOUT:

Grissim, J. Country Music: White Man's Blues; Stambler, I. and Landon, G. Encyclopedia of Folk, Country, and Western Music.

Hoagy Carmichael 1899-

For biographical sketch and list of earlier songs see *Popular American Composers,* 1962.

———

Hoagy Carmichael's hit song "Georgia on My Mind" (1930) was a best seller in 1960-1961 in a recording by Ray Charles for ABC-Paramount; this recording received a Grammy as the best rock 'n' roll release, and another as the best solo male vocal performance of the year.

Carmichael published his second autobiography, *Sometimes I Wonder,* in 1965. The first was *The Stardust Road* (1946), written in collaboration with Stephen Longstreet.

Harry Carroll 1892-1962

For biographical sketch and list of earlier songs see *Popular American Composers,* 1962.

———

Harry Carroll died in Carmel, Pennsylvania, on December 26, 1962.

Ivan Caryll 1861-1921

See *Popular American Composers,* 1962.

Johnny Cash 1932-

JOHNNY CASH has earned the sobriquet of "king of country and western music" both as a singer and as a composer. Many of his own songs deal with poverty, suffering, oppression, the downtrodden, and lost causes. In writing about these and similar subjects he finds his themes in his personal experiences. "Every good song," he has said, "has lived through hard times." And hard times is what Johnny Cash knew for many years.

He was born John R. Cash (the "R" represents no name) in the backwoods country of Arkansas, in Kingsland, on February 26, 1932. He was the fourth of seven children. His father, Ray Cash, was a sharecropper who in 1936 acquired from the Federal land grant twenty acres —with a shack, a barn, and a mule—in Dyess, two hundred miles from Kingsland. There he lived the life of an im-

17

Cash

JOHNNY CASH
Columbia Records

poverished farmer, and there his children were raised.

As a boy, Johnny Cash had to help farm the land behind a plow, pick cotton (some three hundred and fifty pounds a day), and go rabbit hunting—the last not for sport but to supplement the meager diet on the Cash dining table. But Johnny never remembers going hungry, "not real hungry," as he puts it. "I didn't get fat on fancy food a lot of times but I always managed to get enough to eat." When he was fourteen, he helped the family's finances by working as a waterboy for river gangs at a salary of $2.50 a day. His hard childhood was made more difficult when a flood caused damage to the family farm and shack that took months to repair. His boyhood was also touched with tragedy when one of his brothers was accidentally killed in a school workshop.

What made life more or less tolerable for Johnny was singing. Music was a heritage from his maternal grandfather, J. L. Rivers. Despite his own poverty, Rivers owned a guitar, organ, bass viol, and violin. The Rivers household was continually enlivened with music making as neighbors crowded the room not only to listen but also to participate in the singing of hymns. Johnny, as a young child, attended those musicales, and they left a lasting impression on him.

Growing up, Cash was always singing at work and at home. Though they could hardly afford to do so, the Cashes acquired a piano. With the mother providing the accompaniment, the whole family would get their recreation by singing Baptist hymns. (This may be the reason why a certain religious fervor clings to Cash's singing and composing style today.) Johnny also loved listening to country singers on the radio, particularly Hank Williams. When he was twelve, Johnny was writing songs of his own. By the time he attended high school, he was performing over a small radio station in Blytheville, Arkansas, and at school functions. After graduation from high school, Cash worked for a while in a factory in Detroit. But he was soon back home, holding down various menial jobs in town while pursuing his musical interests. When he was seventeen, he won the first prize of five dollars in a local amateur singing contest. He also took singing lessons, paid for by his mother who took in wash to raise the necessary money.

During July of 1950 Cash enlisted in the United States Air Force. He was stationed at Scott Air Force Base in Belleville, Illinois, where he was trained as a radio operator. Here he met and fell in love with Vivian Liberto, his first real romance. The love affair was temporarily interrupted when Cash was shipped off to Germany. During off hours he wrote poems, some of which were published in the *Stars and Stripes*. He also bought a guitar for five dollars (the first time he owned an instrument of his own) and by himself learned how to play it. He would entertain his buddies at the air base besides making appearances in German clubs.

Released from service in June 1954, with the rank of sergeant, Cash returned to the United States. On August 7, 1954, he and Vivian were married by Vivian's uncle, a priest. They made their home in a four-room furnished apartment in Memphis, Tennessee. Hoping to become a disk jockey, Cash took advantage of the G. I. Bill of Rights to study announcing. During the day he supported his wife (who was pregnant with their first child, Rosanne) by selling electrical appliances from door to door. "I was the world's worst salesman," he recalls.

He dropped his course in announcing, abandoned hopes of becoming a disk jockey, and instead tried to make headway as a singer. An audition for Sam Phillips, head of Sun Records, proved a failure when Cash sang hymns. "When you have a different kind of song," Phillips advised him, "let me hear you again."

A significant development in Cash's musical career came with his friendship with Luther Perkins and Marshall Grant. Both were full-time mechanics, and both made music in their spare time. Luther played an amplified guitar, and Marshall, a bass. One day, looking through some of the poems Cash had written while he was in the Air Force, Perkins and Grant suggested he set one or two of them to music. Cash complied, and "Hey, Porter" became the first number in the repertory of the new combo, Johnny Cash and the Tennessee Two. It made its debut at a church social outside Memphis (for a fee of ten dollars), and then performed at various other functions in and around Memphis. At the same time the friends were trying to gain a new audition with Sam Phillips. When it finally materialized, Phillips was so impressed with "Hey, Porter" that he accepted it for recording, but only on the condition that Cash could provide another song for the "flip" side. That night, Cash wrote "Cry, Cry, Cry," which Phillips liked even better than its predecessor. Both songs were recorded for Sun by Johnny Cash and the Tennessee Two and released in June 1955. The recording sold about one hundred thousand disks, reaching the top ten charts within six weeks.

Now under exclusive contract to Sun Records, Cash soon achieved national

fame with "Folsom Prison Blues," which he had written in 1954 after seeing the motion picture *Inside the Walls of Folsom Prison*. Released in 1956 it became Cash's first gold record. He wrote this number in two hours while aboard a plane. "I Walk the Line," also recorded in 1956, became another gold record. This is now one of Cash's best known numbers, the idea having come to him from recollections of his unhappy experiences as a door-to-door salesman. In 1970 the title was used for a motion picture starring Gregory Peck. The background music consisted of Johnny Cash singing his own ballads.

Recordings of "So Doggone Lonesome" and "There You Go" further helped to make Cash one of the hottest new properties in the recording industry and Sam Phillips's most important "find" since Elvis Presley.

His days of poverty were over. Now in constant demand for public performances, recording sessions, interviews, and personal appearances, Cash was a recognized star. "There is nothing forward or demanding about him," wrote Frieda Barter in *Country and Western Jamboree*. "His approach, whether before a mike, before an audience, or with friends, is quiet yet forceful. . . . One actually feels the strength, the warmth and very definitely the sincerity of his personality."

He achieved a unique status in the recording business between 1956 and 1959 when every one of his releases was listed on the top ten charts in the country and western music category. Some of these recordings were of his own songs, some, of songs by others. During these three years he sold over six million records. Recognized by critics, disk jockeys, and the public as one of the top performers and writers of country and western music—and as the star of "The Grand Ole Opry," a radio show devoted to country music broadcast from Nashville, Tennessee—he was now averaging about $250,000 a year. His family was enlarged by three more daughters, and he could afford to buy a ranch-style house on the outskirts of Memphis, one of whose rooms was furnished as his music room and office. He acquired a car, and a dashing new wardrobe. He indulged himself by buying anything that caught his fancy.

By 1960 Cash had written and recorded such all-time Cash favorites as "Next in Line," "Big River," and "Luther Played the Boogie." "Big River" was inspired by the flood that had almost ruined the Cashes when Johnny was a boy; but the immediate stimulus for writing the song came from reading a line in an article about himself that said "Johnny Cash has the Big River blues in his voice." He had the whole song—words and music—clear in his head by the time he finished reading the article.

In 1959 Cash transferred from the Sun label to Columbia Records, with which he was henceforth affiliated. His first Columbia recordings were "Don't Take Your Guns to Town" and the albums *Fabulous Johnny Cash, Ride This Train,* and *Sound of Johnny Cash.* Each was a best seller. During the decade of the 1960's, Cash became one of Columbia's three best-selling artists (he was surpassed in sales only by Barbra Streisand and Johnny Mathis), and was responsible for selling about fifteen million records.

Up to the early 1960's Cash recordings were supplemented by public appearances in America, Europe, Australia, and the Orient. A guest performer on the Ed Sullivan and George Gobel television shows as well as in several television westerns, he was also seen and heard in several motion pictures, including *Five Minutes to Live, The Night Rider* and *Hootenanny.* Indicative of his growing fame was the emergence of Johnny Cash fan clubs throughout the United States. Cash now had two managers to attend to his business interests (which included two publishing houses and real estate investments) and his own press agent.

In the early 1960's a temporary decline in Cash's fortunes and popularity took place, due partly to poor health, partly to overindulgence in tranquilizers and Dexedrine. In 1965 he was jailed for one night in an El Paso prison for carrying Dexedrine tablets across the Mexican border, an experience that further intensified his lifelong sympathy for prisoners, a sympathy he had already voiced in his song "Folsom Prison Blues." "I don't see anything good come out of a prison," he told an interviewer in 1969. "You put them in like animals and tear the souls and guts out of them and let them out worse than when they went in."

It did not take him long to rehabilitate himself, in fact to become even more successful and wealthy than he had been. One of his great triumphs on records, following his rehabilitation, reflected once again his sympathy for prisoners. It was the album *Johnny Cash at Folsom Prison,* a recording of a concert he gave in 1968 for the inmates of that institution. (This was the third time he had sung for the inmates of Folsom Prison since 1962.) The sounds of clanging jail doors, the conversation of the prisoners, announcements over the public address system were allowed to remain in the recording. Over a million of these albums were sold. It received a Grammy as the best male vocal performance of the year and was given the BMI Award as one of the most often performed country and western music records in the repertory. (BMI gave Cash a similar award that year for "I Walk the Line.") A follow-up to *Johnny Cash at Folsom Prison* was the album *Johnny Cash at San Quentin,* and that, too, was a best seller.

In 1970 Cash's "A Boy Named Sue" was not only a leader among Columbia's singles but also a contender for a Grammy as the best single disk of the year and the recipient of the award as the best single disk in the first annual talent award by the Country Music Association of Great Britain. At that time the same association also presented Cash with awards for being the finest country and western entertainer, and the leading singer-on-records of the year.

Other Columbia best sellers in 1970 included, Cash's recording of Kris Kristofferson's "Sunday Morning Coming Down," "Flesh and Blood," and "This Side of Law," and the album *The Johnny Cash Show*. Among his songs recorded by Columbia in 1971 were "You've Got a New Light Shining," "Singing in Viet Nam Talking Blues," "Man in Black," and "Little Bit of Yesterday." In that year his recording with June Carter of "If I Were a Carpenter" received a Grammy as the best country performance by a duo or group.

In 1968 Cash divorced his wife and married June Carter, a talented performer with whom he had been appearing from time to time since 1961. In the fall of that year, Cash gave a concert in Carnegie Hall, New York, that established a box office record there. A concert at Madison Square Garden in New York in December 1968 taxed the capacity of that vast auditorium. "Mr. Cash," reported John S. Wilson in his review in the New York *Times*, "a brilliantly controlled showman, kept his low-keyed delivery just at the throttle's edge—strong enough to rouse his listeners to cheers but never letting it get beyond a warm, easygoing feeling. . . . Mr. Cash . . . made that huge Garden seem intimate and managed to project a feeling of neighborly visiting that is the core of his professional career."

In 1969 Cash was featured in a ninety-minute television documentary entitled *Cash!* which was presented over the NET network on March 16. In a slightly lengthened version it was shown in motion picture theaters in 1970 under the title of *Johnny Cash Onstage and Off*. "The movie was fine on television," reported Roger Greenspun in the New York *Times*, "and it seems to me even better in the theater, where the color is truer, the visual detail finer and the audience situation more properly theatrical." This motion picture follows Cash to some of his concerts (including one in a prison, and another on an Indian reservation); to a recording session with Bob Dylan; to his off-work hours with his children. "He is superb onstage," says Greenspun, "reserved and very decent offstage with his fans (a fine and rigorous uncondescending filming of a meeting with autograph seekers) or with family and friends in Dyess." But Greenspun also found him not so impressive "privately . . . as if he were straining toward a slightly unnatural posture of meditative depth, except when he is with Miss Carter—whose open-featured humorous and intelligent looks work to humanize the Johnny Cash presence and whose musical talent . . . helps to make that presence interesting."

He participated further in motion pictures by singing his songs on the soundtracks of movies, for the already mentioned *I Walk the Line*, and for *Little Fauss and Big Halsy*, both in 1970. In 1971 he wrote and sang the title number of *Gunfight*, a movie in which he co-starred with Kirk Douglas.

Cash's debut in commercial television took place on the ABC network on June 7, 1969. After that, as the star of his own weekly program, he became one of television's major attractions. His television appearances helped to increase his annual income to well beyond two million dollars.

Whether on television or in a public appearance, Cash always opens his program with the simple salutation: "Hello —I'm Johnny Cash." He favors an unusual costume which Albert Govoni says has been "variously described as giving him the appearance of a riverboat gambler, a raffish parson, a card shark out of the Old West, a post—Civil War southern dandy, a New Orleans rakehell on his way to a duel over a woman." His professional dress comprises an outmoded frock coat, gray striped trousers, and a white ruffled-front shirt beneath a vest.

Cash is fascinated by trains, and enjoys such outdoor recreations as fishing, hunting, waterskiing, gardening, and solitary walks in the woods.

ABOUT:

Govoni, A. A Boy Named Cash; Grissim, J. Country Music: White Man's Blues; Hemphill, P. The Nashville Sound: Bright Lights and Country Music.

Life, November 1, 1969; Look, April 29, 1968; Time, June 9, 1969.

George M. Cohan 1878-1942

For biographical sketch and list of earlier songs see *Popular American Composers,* 1962.

_____

On April 10, 1968, a Broadway musical comedy biography of Cohan, entitled *George M!,* was produced with Joel Grey starring as Cohan. The text, little more than a series of vignettes from Cohan's life, served only to introduce Cohan's songs. Some of the songs were, of course, the still familiar standards. But most have long since been forgotten, and two have never even been published. The following Cohan songs were used in this opulent score: "All Aboard for Broadway," "Musical Comedy Man," "Twentieth-Century Love," "My Town," "Billie," "Push Me Along in My Push Cart," "Ring to the Name of Rose," "Popularity," "Give My Regards to Broadway," "Forty-Five Minutes from Broadway," "So Long, Mary," "Down by the Erie," "All Our Friends," "Yankee Doodle Dandy," "Nellie Kelly," "I Love You," "Harrigan," "Over There," "You're a Grand Old Flag," "Dancing Our Worries Away," "The Great Easter Sunday Parade," "Hannah's a Hummer," "Barnum and Bailey Rag," "The Belle of the Barber's Ball," "The American Ragtime," "All in the Wearing," and "I Want to Hear a Yankee Doodle Tune."

Extensively revised and considerably shortened, *George M!* (once again with Joel Grey as star) was telecast coast to coast in 1970.

Cy Coleman 1929-

CY COLEMAN was born Cy Kaufman in the Bronx, New York, on June 14, 1929. He was a musical prodigy, who, at the age of four could correctly reproduce on the piano tunes he had heard. Two years later, after studying with local teachers, he gave recitals at Steinway Hall and Town Hall in New York City. His talent was recognized by the Music Education League which for three consecutive years (1934 through 1936) gave him the Interborough Award.

While still attending the High School of Music and Art he also enrolled at the New York College of Music, which he left in 1948. After that he studied music privately with Rudolph Gruen, Adele Marcus, and Bernard Wagenaar. Meanwhile, as a teenager, he played the piano in servicemen's clubs, a job which was instrumental in drawing him from serious to popular music. After graduating from high school in 1947 he formed a popular music trio which made its debut at the Little Club in New York, and later played at various other nightspots. After appearing on the *DuMont Hour* on television, Coleman continued to work for both radio and television for about a decade, but as a composer rather than as a performer. His most important assignments were: *Date in Manhattan* on NBC in 1948; the *Kate Smith Show* on NBC in 1951 and 1952; and *Art Ford's Village Party* on WNEW (radio) in 1957 and 1958.

Coleman began writing popular songs in the early 1950's with Joseph A. McCarthy as lyricist. In 1952 they wrote "I'm Gonna Laugh You Out of My Life" (subsequently popularized by Nat "King" Cole in a Capitol recording) and "Why Try to Change Me Now," introduced by Frank Sinatra. A third Coleman-McCarthy song, "Tin Pan Alley," marked Coleman's debut in the Broadway theater. This song was used as the first-act finale of John Murray Anderson's *Almanac* in 1953. In 1956 Tony Bennett (who would

CY COLEMAN

henceforth be identified with numerous Coleman hit songs) made a recording of "The Autumn Waltz" (lyrics by Bob Hilliard). A year later Coleman wrote the incidental music for, and served as the musical director of, *Compulsion*, a nonmusical Broadway production.

The year 1957 proved eventful, as far as Coleman's progress as a popular composer was concerned, when he began his collaboration with the lyricist Carolyn Leigh. Miss Leigh had worked as a copywriter for an advertising firm, had contributed material for radio shows, and was the lyricist for several songs used in a Broadway production of *Peter Pan* starring Mary Martin. Coleman knew her only casually, but greeting her in the street one day in 1957, he suggested they work together. In two days' time they had their first song on paper, "A Moment of Madness." It was both published and recorded (the latter by Sammy Davis, Jr.). From then on a permanent working arrangement was decided upon, which in time yielded twenty published songs (many of them outstanding hits), scores for two Broadway musicals, and several songs for motion pictures.

In 1957 they wrote "Good Intentions," "I Walk a Little Faster," "My How the

Time Goes By," and a remarkable song success, "Witchcraft," first heard in Julius Monk's nightclub revue *Take Five*. It was Frank Sinatra, in a recording, who provided the momentum that swept this song to the height of popularity.

Their hit song of 1958 was "Firefly," written to audition for the job of writing the score for a forthcoming Broadway musical *Gypsy*. That choice assignment went to Jule Styne and Stephen Sondheim, but the disappointment was diluted when "Firefly," in Tony Bennett's recording, became a best seller. Also during 1958, a Tony Bennett recording once again helped make a success of a Coleman-Leigh number—"It Amazes Me." Before the year ended the songwriters had produced "Hibiscus" (introduced by Jo Stafford), "Now I Lay Me Down to Sleep," and "You Fascinate Me So." The last two were introduced in Julius Monk's *Demi-Dozen*, another nightclub revue.

Tony Bennett recorded two new Coleman-Leigh numbers in 1959, "The Best Is Yet to Come" and "Marry Young." This was also the year in which "The Tempo of the Times" was introduced in a nightclub revue, *Medium Rare*. In 1960 "Playboy Theme" was written for and used in the TV series, *Playboy Penthouse Party*.

Coleman and Leigh wrote their first full score for a Broadway musical in 1960: *Wildcat*, a show tailor-made for Lucille Ball in her return to the stage. *Wildcat*, which opened on December 16, 1960, starred Miss Ball in the hardly glamorous role of a wildcat promoter. During most of the production she wore only dirty dungarees and a blue shirt. But she held her audiences with her personal magnetism and gift for comedy, and in fact she proved to be the sole interest that this musical held for audiences. When she decided to leave the production, it folded after only 171 performances. The score had a major hit in "Hey, Look Me Over", a number which Miss Ball shared with Paula Stewart. This melody (with specially written new lyrics by

Coleman

Miss Leigh) was used to promote the mayoralty campaign in New York of Louis J. Lefkowitz and after that for Edward M. Kennedy in his Massachusetts primary fight with Edward J. McCormack for the Democratic senatorial nomination.

Before returning to the Broadway theater, Coleman and Leigh added another hit to their chain of song sucesses —"The Rules of the Road," recorded by Tony Bennett.

Their Broadway return came with *Little Me* (the first musical for which Neil Simon wrote a script). Opening on November 17, 1962, it had a run of 257 performances. Sid Caesar was starred as a number of characters, all of whom become involved in the life of Belle Poitrine, whose life and love affairs are traced from her days of dire poverty to her reign as a movie queen. The outstanding song in this production was "Real Live Girl."

Little Me was the last Broadway musical on which Coleman collaborated with Carolyn Leigh. Their last song hits were heard in 1964: "When in Rome," successfully recorded by Barbra Streisand, and "Pass Me By," written for the film *Father Goose* but popularized by Peggy Lee.

While working, Coleman and Leigh lived near one another in separate houses in East Hampton, Long Island. Songs came into being only after a good deal of discussion, argument, and at times violent disagreement. "It's the best way for us," Miss Leigh told Whitney Bolton. "He writes a song and plays it for me and I don't like it and I say, 'Cy, no, I won't write for *that*.'" Or, on the other hand, Miss Leigh brought her lyrics to Coleman only to be told: "I've known you to do much better on a bad day for creation. Try again, poet, try again. I wouldn't link eight notes to that if it were the last lyric on earth." What followed was a good deal of careful planning, writing, rewriting, revising, and polishing by composer and lyricist until both were satisfied.

When the Coleman and Leigh partnership ended, the composer teamed up with a veteran lyricist, Dorothy Fields. One of their earlier efforts was the song "Baby Dream Your Dream" in 1966. With the Broadway musical *Sweet Charity*, they achieved a major stage success and Coleman's first moneymaking Broadway show. Based on the Italian motion picture *Nights of Cabiria*, which Neil Simon adapted into a stage musical, *Sweet Charity* came to Broadway on January 29, 1966, and stayed for over 600 performances. After that, a national company took it throughout America, and in 1969 it was made by Universal into a motion picture starring Shirley MacLaine in the role originated on the stage by Gwen Verdon. Both played the part of Charity Hope Valentine, a dance hostess with a heart of gold and an unshakable faith in the goodness of people. She is ever in search of the grand romance of her life, only to be continually frustrated or disillusioned. The leading song-and-dance number was "If My Friend Could See Me Now," in a gifted and varied score that included "There's Gotta Be Something Better Than This," "I'm a Brass Band," "Where Am I Going?" and "Baby, Dream Your Dream." When *Sweet Charity* became a movie, Cy Coleman did his own scoring which earned him an Academy Award nomination in 1970.

Coleman's additional chores for the screen included background music for *The Art of Love* (from which came the song "So Long, Baby") and *Walk, Don't Run* (for which he wrote the title song, sung by Peggy Lee on the film credit soundtrack and recorded by her).

In 1969 Coleman wrote an instrumental number, *Russian Roulette*. A year later he and Fields completed the score for a new Broadway musical, *Eleanor*, based on the romance of Eleanor and Franklin Delano Roosevelt. The text follows them from the time when Roosevelt was attending Harvard through their courtship and marriage and ends with Roosevelt's decision to enter politics.

ABOUT:
ASCAP Biographical Dictionary (1966).

Con Conrad 1891-1938

See *Popular American Composers,* 1962.

J. Fred Coots 1897-

See *Popular American Composers,* 1962.

H. P. Danks 1834-1903

See *Popular American Composers,* 1962.

Bobby Darin 1936-

THOUGH Bobby Darin is best known as a rock 'n' roll singer, and as a motion picture actor, he has also achieved renown as a popular composer. When he was born in Harlem, New York, on May 14, 1936, he was named Walden Robert Cassotto, which he changed to Bobby Darin when he launched his professional career. (He picked the surname by flipping the pages of a telephone book.)

His father, a cabinetmaker, died a few months before Bobby's birth. Bobby knew the full meaning of poverty from infancy on. His crib was a large-sized cardboard carton. He was raised by his mother (a former vaudevillian) and an older sister. A sickly child who had to be fed goat's milk, he suffered recurring attacks of rheumatic fever for five consecutive years beginning when he was eight. Bobby's sickness further intensified the family's financial problems. They had to subsist for the most part on home relief in a cold-water flat in the Bronx.

Darin's poor health made it impossible for him to attend grade school. Exceedingly bright, he was able to make up for this lost schooling through intensive reading and through lessons given him by his mother. When he finally attended school (junior high school) he proved an outstanding student. During this time he taught himself to play the piano, guitar, vibraphone, drums, and

BOBBY DARIN

bass. In 1953 he was graduated from the Bronx High School of Science with honors.

He enrolled in Hunter College, where he specialized in speech and drama courses. Impatient to make a career in the theater, however, he left college without a degree and unsuccessfully tried getting a job on Broadway. He supported himself by making random appearances in small nightspots in New York and by playing the drums during the summer in resorts in the Catskill Mountains. In the mountains he was required occasionally to fill in as singer, master of ceremonies, and busboy. Winters, when engagements were unavailable, he swept the floors in a metal factory and cleaned guns for the Navy.

For a time he collaborated with Don Krishner (who later became a music publisher) in writing singing commercials for the radio. With the money thus earned, Darin and Krishner cut two demonstration records which brought them a one-year contract with Decca Records in March of 1956, their first release being "Dealer in Dreams." In the same year, Darin made his television debut on the *Tommy Dorsey Show,* billed as "the nineteen-year-old singing sensation." When

25

his contract with Decca expired he signed another one-year agreement, this time with a new firm, Atco Records.

One day, visiting a friend, he heard his friend's mother remark jokingly that Darin should be writing a song called "Splish, Splash, Takin' a Bath." More in jest than in earnest, Darin collaborated with Jean Murray on a rock 'n' roll number, "Splish Splash," which Darin recorded for Atco in 1958. It sold a hundred thousand disks in three weeks, and in time became Darin's first recording to pass the million-copy mark. It was also responsible for making him an idol of the teenage set. He followed this recording with that of "Queen of the Hop," which he wrote to Woody Harris's lyrics, "This Little Girl's Gone Rockin'," words by Mann Curtis, and "Dream Lover" to his own lyrics. "Dream Lover" and "Queen of the Hop" became gold records.

Dissatisfied to have only teenage followers, Darin sought out a wider audience by financing the recording of an album, *That's All*, of familiar song favorites by other writers. One of the numbers was "Mack the Knife" from the Bertolt Brecht–Kurt Weill musical play *The Threepenny Opera* (which had been revived Off Broadway with great success). *That's All* sold half a million albums. But a single by Darin of "Mack the Knife" accumulated a sale of well over two million disks, placing number one on the bestseller lists for nine consecutive weeks. In addition, this record received two Grammy awards, one for Darin as the year's best singer. Ed Sullivan now called Darin "the greatest rhythm singer in the world." Walter Winchell described him as "the best singer since Jolson." One year later, Bobby Darin shared with Johnny Mathis the honor of being chosen the top male singer in a teenage poll conducted by the Gilbert Youth Research Company.

The man who had convinced Darin and Atco Records to release "Mack the Knife" as a single was Steve Blauner who, in 1959, became Darin's manager. Through his efforts, Darin assumed a commanding position among America's younger singing stars, with guest appearances on major television programs and public performances in nightclubs and hotels. In 1959 he made his nightclub debut at The Cloister in Hollywood, following it with appearances with George Burns at The Sahara in Las Vegas. On June 2, 1960, Darin made a sensational New York nightclub debut at the Copacabana. Barclay Hudson reported in the New York *World-Telegram* that Darin "has a driving, pulsating style which, combined with an impish, small-boy smile, made him irresistible to his fans." Concert and nightclub appearances in Europe and Australia followed. In January of 1961 Darin headlined as the youngest performer to star on his own one-hour television special: "Bobby Darin and His Friends," over the NBC network. During 1961 his song "Things" became another of his records to exceed a million-copy sale. He was now earning more than half a million dollars a year.

Darin's motion picture debut also took place in 1961, when he appeared in *Come September* as a young American on vacation in southern Europe with several other teenagers. For this movie Darin also wrote and sang both the title song and "Multiplication." By 1962 four more motion pictures starred Darin: *Too Late Blues, Hell Is for Heroes, State Fair,* and *Pressure Point. State Fair* was the remake of an old-time Rodgers and Hammerstein screen musical. In *Pressure Point*, Darin played the part of a Nazi in a straight dramatic role. His recording of the title song which he wrote and sang in *If a Man Answers* became a best seller (this time on the Capitol label to which Darin had transferred in January of 1962 on a long-term contract). Another hit song from this picture was his adaptation of its love theme into "A True, True Love."

Among the motion pictures in which Bobby Darin appeared subsequently and for which he also wrote the title songs were *The Lively Set, That Funny Feeling,* and *Gunfight in Abilene.* For *The Lively*

Set he also wrote "If You Love Him" and for *Gunfight in Abilene* the background music. In *The Happy Ending,* Bobby Darin appeared as a gigolo in Nassau, and in the Walt Disney production *That Darn Cat* he sang a number.

During the filming of *Come September,* Darin fell in love with Sandra Dee, who was also in the cast. They were married on December 1, 1960; a son, Dodd Mitchell Cassotto, was born to them a year later. Bobby Darin and Sandra Dee were costarred in several movies including *That Funny Feeling* in 1964. They were subsequently divorced.

Some other songs by Darin—many of them among his hit recordings—are "Love Me Right," "Delia," "By My Side," "You're the Reason I'm Living," "Eighteen Yellow Roses," "Jailer, Bring Me Water," and "Two of a Kind." For the last of these Johnny Mercer provided the lyrics. Bobby Darin's first album for Capitol, *Oh! Look at Me Now,* in 1962, was an immediate best seller.

Darin has remained a favorite in nightclubs and hotels. In 1963, he appeared at the Flamingo Hotel in Las Vegas. He was such a draw that the hotel signed him to a four-year contract valued at a million dollars. His first appearance under this arrangement established new attendance records for the Flamingo Hotel with almost 43,000 patrons taxing its capacity each evening for four weeks.

In 1958 Darin bought a house in Lake Hiawatha, New Jersey, where he lived with his sister and mother until he married Sandra Dee. After his marriage, he made his home in Beverly Hills, California. His annual income is now well over a million dollars.

For many years Darin was known as the "angry young man" of show business because of his combustible temper, his brash and cocky manner, and his habit of speaking out straight from the shoulder. About his personal life he has always been tight-lipped, another characteristic that did not endear him to the press. In later years he mellowed considerably but without suppressing that dynamism and electricity that made him a star.

Early in 1971 Darin underwent heart surgery in Los Angeles.

ABOUT:
Stambler, I. Encyclopedia of Popular Music.
McCall's Magazine, October 1961; Saturday Evening Post, May 6, 1961.

Reginald De Koven 1859-1920

See *Popular American Composers,* 1962.

Peter De Rose 1900-1953

For biographical sketch and list of earlier songs see *Popular American Composers,* 1962.

––––––

Peter De Rose's song classic, "Deep Purple," again became a best seller in 1963 in a recording by Nino Tempo and April Stevens that received a Grammy as the best rock 'n' roll record of the year.

Antoine ("Fats") Domino 1928-

IN THE EARLY history of rock 'n' roll, the name and music of "Fats" Domino occupy a place of singular importance. Extraordinarily prolific and successful, he proved a powerful influence in crystallizing the rock 'n' roll style that would dominate the music industry.

Domino was born in New Orleans, Louisiana, on February 26, 1928, one of nine children (and the only one with a talent for music). His father was an amateur violinist. As a boy, he became fascinated with the blues and ragtime music then so popular in New Orleans. He was only five when he began picking out similar tunes on the battered piano a kindly cousin had given the family. Noting the boy's interest in music, an uncle began teaching him to use chords—all the formal instruction he ever received.

27

Domino

"FATS" DOMINO
Warner Bros. Reprise Records

In early boyhood Domino began earning pennies playing ragtime and the blues during the weekends in honky-tonks in or near New Orleans. The rest of the week he worked in a bedspring factory. An accident in that factory almost brought his musical career to an end when a spring fell on his hand and crushed it. For a time it appeared he would never again play the piano. With a remarkable strength of will and with infinite patience young Domino began exercising his fingers for hours every day until their one-time flexibility was restored and he could resume playing the piano.

At nineteen Domino was hired by a jazz band; this job lasted two weeks. He then organized a band of his own which performed three times a week at the Hideaway Club in New Orleans; his salary was three dollars a week. To supplement this he took a job in a lumber mill.

Word of his musical ability and personal style as jazz pianist began to circulate until it reached the ears of Lew Chudd, who had just founded Imperial Records. Chudd came to the Hideaway Club, heard Domino, and signed him to a contract. Domino's first recording, in 1948, was his own number "The Fat Man," intended to be self-descriptive.

This record sold a million disks. Having started his composing and recording career so triumphantly, Domino proceeded to become one of the most successful creators of rock 'n' roll music in recording history. For some of his numbers he wrote both the words and the music; others were written in collaboration with Dave Bartholomew; a few represented a joint effort by Domino and various writers. His second million-disk sale came in 1952 with "Goin' Home" (written with A. E. Young). His third, fourth, fifth, and sixth records to sell a million or more copies all appeared in 1953: "Goin' to the River," "You Said You Loved Me," and "I Lived My Life" (all three in collaboration with Bartholomew); and "Please Don't Leave Me" (words and music by Domino). Within a dozen years after his first recorded song Domino had sold about sixty million single disks and four million albums, and had achieved twenty-two gold records. Only two other recording artists achieved more gold records than Domino—Bing Crosby and Elvis Presley. The majority of Domino's gold records were of his own songs, written by himself or in collaboration with others. Two came in 1954, "Love Me" and "Don't Leave Me This Way"; three in 1955, "Ain't That a Shame," "All By Myself," and "I Can't Go On"; three in 1956, "Boll Weevil," "I'm in Love Again," and "Blue Monday"; three in 1957, "I'm Walking," "It's You I Love," and "I Still Love You"; one in 1958 (though the millionth disk was not sold until 1960), "Whole Lotta Lovin' "; one in 1959, "Be My Guest"; and two in 1960, "Walkin' to New Orleans" and "Don't Come Knockin'." Most of Domino's own songs were inspired by personal everyday experiences or chance remarks he overheard.

The strong pulse and dynamic drive of Domino's songs, whether or not written in collaboration, are always made more effective in his own performance. He sings in a raspy voice and plays the piano with a pounding style. Both help to emphasize the beat and to accentuate the original sweep of the melodic line. Domino thus became outstandingly successful not only on records but also in public appearances in nightclubs and hotels, over radio and television, and occasionally in motion pictures. In the motion picture *The Girl Can't Help It* (1956) he sang his own "Blue Monday."

Domino continued to make numerous recordings in the 1960's, both singles and albums, including songs by other composers. Among his best albums were *Here Comes Fats, Fats on Fire, Getaway with Fats, Stompin' Fats Domino,* and *Fats Is Back.* But his popularity both as a recording artist and as a composer went into sharp decline as new sounds and styles began dominating the field of rock 'n' roll. Nevertheless, nostalgia for the older era of rock 'n' roll made it possible for him to attract a huge audience in a personal appearance at the Brooklyn Paramount in 1968, and later in Central Park and at Fillmore East, both in New York. In the last of these appearances, in 1970, he sang many of his biggest hits supported by five instrumentalists. "Mr. Domino's songs have become a landmark, and it was good to hear them done," said Mike Jahn in the New York *Times.*

ABOUT:

Feather, L. The New Edition of the Encyclopedia of Jazz; Roxon, L. Rock Encyclopedia; Stambler, I. Encyclopedia of Popular Music.

Walter Donaldson 1893-1947

See *Popular American Composers,* 1962.

Ervin Drake 1919-

ERVIN MAURICE DRAKE was born in New York City on April 3, 1919. Music played a negligible part in his early life. He attended the New York City public schools and was graduated from the College of the City of New York with a Bachelor of Science degree in 1940. In college, his main interests were English literature, graphic arts (including life drawing, painting, and lithography), and now, for the first time, music. His extracurricular activities included contributing cartoons, humor, and art to the college humor magazine, *Mercury,* of which he later became editor, and composing music for several varsity productions. Some of his popular songs were published by important companies, and a few of his cartoons appeared in several national-circulation magazines, including *The Saturday Evening Post* and *Collier's.*

Upon graduation from college he was faced with choosing a career, and his father induced him to go into the wholesale furniture business. However, music was assuming an increasingly important place among his interests. He reinforced his still meager musical knowledge by studying theory, composition, and orchestration with Tibor Serly; he followed this with an extension course in orchestration at the Juilliard School of Music. His instrument was the piano, which he used extensively for his compositions. (During 1969, however, he started studying both the classical acoustic guitar and the new electric variety. Since then he has indulged himself in "the luxury of composing music on a different instrument. It feels like a second-stage rocket. My instructor, Jack Hotop, is a leading recording guitarist.")

Show business fascinated him. He felt that an important step in that direction would be developing a career as a writer of popular songs, and he produced a repertory of numbers (words as well as music) before achieving his first two hits, both in 1943. One was "Tico-Tico," a popular Brazilian melody for which he wrote English lyrics. It was introduced in a cartoon film, *Saludos Amigos*; later Xavier Cugat and his orchestra performed it in the motion picture *Bathing Beauty* (1944), and Ethel Smith, the

Drake

ERVIN DRAKE

organist, popularized it and made it her theme number. Since then, "Tico-Tico" has been featured in several major films and has established itself as a standard.

His other hit song of 1943, for which Drake wrote his own melody as well as the words, was "The Rickety Rickshaw Man," which sold a million disks in 1946 (Eddie Howard's second big record).

Drake extended his fame as songwriter before the 1940's ended. In 1944 (with H. J. Lengsfelder) he wrote the English lyrics for "Perdido," a jazz melody formerly introduced by Duke Ellington and his orchestra which became a jazz classic. "Good Morning, Heartache," written with Dan Fisher and Irene Higginbotham in 1946, was made famous by Billie Holiday. In 1947 Drake collaborated with Jimmy Shirl on the English words for a Brazilian melody that became celebrated as "Come to the Mardi Gras." In the same year "Sonata" (words and music by Drake) was a million-disk seller in Perry Como's recording. Other Drake songs were heard in the motion pictures *Holiday in Mexico, The Arch of Triumph,* and *Across the Missouri,* for the last of which he wrote the title song.

The 1950's and 1960's comprised the period of Drake's biggest hit songs. "Be-

loved, Be Faithful," written with Jimmy Shirl in 1950, and performed by Russ Morgan and his orchestra, became a bestselling record and the number one song in England that Christmas; it did almost as well in France. "Castle Rock" (lyrics in collaboration with Jimmy Shirl), a pioneer rock 'n' roll number in 1951, was popularized in a recording by Frank Sinatra accompanied by Harry James and his orchestra. This was followed by Drake's song triumph, "I Believe," written in 1952 with Jimmy Shirl, Al Stillman, and Irvin Graham for Jane Froman who introduced it on her TV production, *USA Canteen,* over the CBS network. Frankie Laine, who recorded it in 1953, was largely responsible for making it the most successful song of the year, according to the number of times it was represented on the *Hit Parade;* the song was the recipient of the Christopher Award. "My Friend" (written with Jimmy Shirl) was an inspirational ballad which became a favorite of Eddie Fisher's in 1954. In England it was the top seller in a Frankie Laine record made especially for release there; when Frankie Laine sang it at the Palladium he brought down the house.

Drake's major song in the 1960's was "It Was a Very Good Year" (1961), first recorded by the Kingston Trio, then by various other folk singers. It took four years for this number to achieve its formidable popularity, and this came about through Frank Sinatra's immensely successful rendition on records, over TV, and in nightclubs. In the 1960's Drake also wrote "The New Old Oaken Bucket"; "Al Di Là" (his English lyrics adapted for an Italian melody); and "Father of the Girls" (lyrics inspired by Drake's own experience with daughters) which Perry Como made into a hit record.

Television heavily engaged Drake's activity from 1948 to 1962. He served at various times as writer, composer, associate producer, and producer—sometimes in several capacities for the same show. He had a hand in some seven hundred telecasts during this period. Most of his programs were in a series, such as the *Jane Froman Show, The Big Record* (starring Patti Page), the *Frankie Laine Show*, the *Merv Griffin Show,* the *Teresa Brewer Show,* the *Mel Tormé Show,* and others. Drake worked on numerous specials involving such stars as Ethel Merman, Steve Lawrence and Eydie Gormé, and Gene Kelly, among others. Major TV productions to which he looks back with considerable pride are the birthday salute to Mrs. Dwight D. Eisenhower (carried by both CBS and ABC networks), for which he supplied both the script and the song "To Mamie with Music"; and *The Bachelor,* starring Hal March, Carol Haney, Jayne Mansfield, and Julie Wilson. He contributed the songs and served as associate producer for this TV show. Both these productions took place in 1956, the latter earning Drake Sylvania Awards as songwriter and producer. From 1960 to 1962 his most significant TV productions were *Accent on Love,* starring Mike Nichols and Elaine May with Gower Champion and Ginger Rogers in 1960; *Yves Montand on Broadway,* in 1961; nominated that year for an Emmy Award; and in 1962 the *Timex Comedy Hour,* hosted by Johnny Carson, which received the top audience rating for a variety special.

Drake wrote the words and music for the songs to the successful Broadway musical *What Makes Sammy Run?,* which opened on Broadway on February 27, 1964. This was an adaptation of Budd Shulberg's novel of the same name—a devastating portrait of Hollywood and of a young opportunist with a ruthless drive to become a major producer. The part of the opportunist, Sammy Glick, was played by Steve Lawrence, the singer, in his Broadway stage debut; he received top honors in the New York Drama Critics poll for the best male performer in a Broadway musical. Drake's score boasted several fine songs, among them "My Hometown," "A Room Without Windows," and "Something to Live For."

A second Broadway musical, produced in 1968 with lyrics and music by Drake, proved far less successful. It was *Her First Roman,* a musical adaptation of Bernard Shaw's *Caesar and Cleopatra,* costarring Richard Kiley and Leslie Uggams. It had just seventeen performances. The principal songs were "Just for Today," "In Vino Veritas," "The Wrong Man," and "I Cannot Make Him Jealous."

Besides writing songs for Broadway, Drake composed the music for a number of motion pictures in the 1950's and 1960's, among these *Foreign Intrigue, Affair at the Villa Fiorita, Rome Adventure,* and *Two for the Guillotine.*

On May 28, 1947, Drake married Ada Sax. They and their four daughters live in Great Neck, Long Island. Drake maintains an office in New York. His hobbies include painting and golf. He says: "My paintings fall somewhere between poor and fair. At golf I am enthusiastic but dreadful, having broken ninety only three times in my life. I once got a hole-in-one, which, considering the level of my game, indicates how much luck there is in all fields of endeavor."

ABOUT:
ASCAP Biographical Dictionary (1966).

Paul Dresser 1857-1906

See *Popular American Composers,* 1962.

Vernon Duke 1903-1969

For biographical sketch and list of earlier songs see *Popular American Composers,* 1962.

———

Vernon Duke's last two produced stage musicals, *Zenda* and *Pink Jungle,* expired out of town before reaching Broadway. *Cabin in the Sky* (1940), revived Off Broadway in January 1964, was a box office failure. It included a new song written specifically for this revival, "Living It Up" (words and music by Duke), together with two numbers discarded from the original 1940 Broadway production, "My Old Virginia Home on the River" and "We'll Live All Over Again."

An important activity for Duke before his death was translating lyrics of American popular songs into Russian for transmission to the Soviet Union over Radio Liberty. Just before his death, Duke was working on a score for a musical based on Mark Twain's life.

Duke was operated on for a tumor of the lung on January 8, 1969. He died of cardiac arrest on January 16, after a second tumor operation.

Bob Dylan 1941-

BOB DYLAN
Courtesy Columbia Records

BOB DYLAN began his career as a composer by writing folksongs. Had he continued permanently in this direction he would not have been included in this volume which is devoted exclusively to creators of popular music. But following his success in the folk idiom, he evolved a style of composition in which folk and rock elements were combined—a style for which the term "folk rock" was coined. This development moves him into the realm of popular music.

Born Robert Zimmerman in Duluth, Minnesota, on May 21, 1941, Dylan was one of three sons of an impoverished appliance dealer. The family moved to the neighboring town of Hibbing when Bob was still a child. This was such a poor community that the family soon went on to South Hibbing with the hope that opportunities for the father to make a living could be improved. There Bob attended public schools. Hating the town, school, and his family life, Bob Dylan ran away from home for the first time when he was ten years old. He returned to South Hibbing, but left home no less than six times in the next eight years, traveling as far as California by hitching rides, jumping on boxcars, or walking.

Dylan was a musical child whose first significant influence came from hearing a Negro blues singer and guitarist. This made such an impression on the boy that, in his own efforts to make music, he would sing songs while beating out rhythms by banging two spoons together as if they were castanets. Whenever he came upon a street singer he would listen spellbound. One of them gave him an old, battered guitar which he learned to play well enough to be able to accompany himself in his songs.

When Dylan was eleven, he heard the veteran blues singer Big Joe Williams. This was an unforgettable experience, and a decisive one as far as Dylan's development as a musician was concerned. As he later remembered: "The way I think about the blues tune comes from what I learned from Big Joe Williams. . . . But what makes the real blues singers so great is that they are able to state all the problems they had; but at the same time, they were standing outside of them and could look at them."

Despite his absences from home and school, Dylan managed to graduate from Hibbing High School. There he formed a rock 'n' roll band, his passion for rock 'n' roll having been stimulated by listening to local radio broadcasts of the records of Chuck Berry, "Fats" Domino, and others. By this time he had learned to play not only the guitar but also the piano, harmonica, and autoharp. As a member of a traveling carnival, which he had joined when he was thirteen, he appeared as a singer with his own guitar accompaniment. He was also writing songs; the subject of his first ballad was Brigitte Bardot. It was during high school days that he decided to change his name to "Dylan," naming himself after his favorite poet, Dylan Thomas.

After high school, Bob Dylan worked as folk singer in a striptease dive in Central City, Colorado, where he filled in when the girls were offstage. He retained this job just a week and a half, since his audience, far more interested in girls than in singing, expressed its dissatisfaction with Dylan in no uncertain terms. Discouraged by this unfortunate experience, he decided to settle down for more education. He enrolled in the University of Minnesota on a scholarship in 1960, but his academic life lasted just six months. "I sat in science," as he subsequently wrote in one of his free-verse poems, "My Life in a Stolen Moment," "an' flunked out for refusin' to watch a rabbit die. I got expelled from English class for using four-letter words in a paper describing the English teacher." During this brief stay at the University he worked during off-school hours singing with a folksong group at a local coffeehouse.

By the time Dylan was through permanently with formal education, he had come under the greatest single musical influence of his life, that of Woody Guthrie, the folk singer, with whose recordings he had become thoroughly familiar. Guthrie's poignant songs of protest about migrant workers, refugees, and victims of a privileged society moved him to write the same kind of folksongs. He, too, during his extended wanderings around the United States, had experienced suffering, injustice, social inequality, and the inhumanity of which some people were capable. Bob Dylan's admiration of Woody Guthrie grew when he at-tended one of Guthrie's concerts in Carmel, California, an event that he found profoundly moving. Some time later, Dylan met Guthrie for the only time. Guthrie was wasting away from the hereditary disease that eventually killed him, and Dylan visited him in a hospital. The sight of his idol, withered and dying, strengthened Dylan in his determination to follow Guthrie as a singer and creator of folksongs with a message.

When Dylan left home for the last time (at eighteen) he headed for New York. He made music in local coffeehouses for such a pittance that he had to seek shelter at night either in subways or at a friend's apartment; often he went through an entire day without eating. The real meaning of personal suffering was now forcefully brought home to him; he dwelt frequently on the subject of suffering in the songs he was writing. In his public appearances he wore the same threadbare, shabby, and often dirty clothes that had to serve him when he was not on the stage. He accompanied himself on a guitar, but sometimes interrupted his singing to play the harmonica (which was attached to his neck by a wire) and to make commentaries on a variety of subjects in an unschooled, ungrammatical drawl. His singing was also rough and uncouth.

Dylan might have continued indefinitely leading the vagrant life of a homeless and hungry balladeer, singing for the pennies and nickels his audience doled out to him, if he had not been discovered by the folk-music critic of the New York *Times*, Robert Shelton. Shelton heard Dylan at Gerde's Folk City on Fourth Street in Greenwich Village. He was taken aback by the unique personal style of both the singer and his songs. Shelton wrote on September 29, 1961: "A bright new face in folk music is appearing at Gerde's Folk City. Although only twenty years old, Bob Dylan is one of the most distinctive stylists to play in a Manhattan cabaret in months. Resembling a cross between a choirboy and a

33

beatnik, Mr. Dylan has a cherubic look and a mop of tousled hair he partly covers with a Huck Finn black corduroy cap. His clothes may need a bit of tailoring. But when he works his guitar, harmonica, or piano and composes new songs faster than he can remember them, there is no doubt that he is bursting at the seam with talent."

This flattering notice brought Dylan an offer from Columbia Records to make his first album, *Bob Dylan*. It was the only album he ever recorded in which none of his own songs was represented. On November 4, 1961, Dylan gave his first concert at the Carnegie Chapter Hall in New York.

By 1962 he was beginning to earn enough through his singing to rent his own apartment on West Fourth Street for eighty dollars a month, eat regularly, and find the leisure and peace of mind to write an endless stream of songs and poems. Out of this mass came the song that started him on the road to fame and prosperity, "Blowin' in the Wind." In it, intolerance, injustice, bigotry, exploitation, war, and other evils are touched upon symbolically in verse, while the music has a simple, haunting folk quality whose impact comes from oft-repeated melodic phrases. This was one of two of Dylan's own songs included in his second Columbia album, *The Freewheelin' Bob Dylan*, released in 1962. That album sold well. But what made "Blowin' in the Wind" one of the most successful songs of 1962-1963 was a recording by Peter, Paul and Mary which sold almost two million disks and received two Grammy awards, one as the best folk recording of the year, the other as the best performance by a vocal group. The song was even adopted by the integration movement. It was a sensation when featured at the Newport Folk Festival in 1962; such celebrated folk singers as Joan Baez and Peter Seeger came onstage to join Bob Dylan in singing it. After that the song was recorded by over fifty different vocal groups.

As for the album, *The Freewheelin' Bob Dylan,* a reviewer for *High Fidelity* wrote: "Bob Dylan's gifts lie not in an attractive vocalism but rather in his ability to pen folklike songs of social protest. . . . He does pinpoint the stresses and outrages of our tortured era. . . . Dylan's vocal style strikes me as fifty percent true hillbilliness and fifty percent unmitigated phoniness, but it is worth enduring for the songs which so unerringly crystallize the fears and failures of a world that, increasingly, is too much with all of us."

The racial problem continued to concern Bob Dylan in numbers like "Ballad of Emmett Till" (the black boy who was lynched in Mississippi because he whistled at a white woman) and "Only a Pawn in Their Game" (inspired by the murder of Medgar Evers, the civil rights leader). But other social, political, and international problems were treated in his songs as his popularity, and the sales of his records, kept growing. In 1963 he wrote "When the Ship Comes In," an expression of despair at what the future holds for the world; "The Times They Are A-Changin'," touching on the generation gap; "Masters of War," an indictment of munitions manufacturers; "Ballad of Hollis Brown," the story of a man so desperate that he murdered his entire family; "Hard Rain's A-Gonna Fall," about the threat of nuclear war; "Don't Think Twice, It's All Right," about the sexual revolution; and "With God on Our Side," a devastating attack upon war.

The next two years brought another rich harvest of songs of which these are representative: "The Lonesome Death of Hattie Carroll," "Lay Down Your Weary Tune" (a tribute to Woody Guthrie), "My Back Pages," "It Ain't Me, Babe," "I Don't Believe You," "Restless Farewell," "Chimes of Freedom," "Black Crow Blues," "All I Really Want to Do," "Baby, You Been on My Mind," "I Shall Be Free," "All Grown Up," "Talking World War III," "Who Killed Davey

Moore?," "If You Got to Go, Go," and "Gates of Eden."

"Dylan," wrote Burt Korall in the *Saturday Review*, "caught the tenor of the times. Innocence was a thing of the past. . . . He realized that isolation from true reality was as unbearable as the reality itself. Yet this did not prohibit him from immersing himself in a surrealistic pessimism." In a subsequent issue of the *Saturday Review*, Steven Goldberg said: "Dylan does not teach, neither does he proselytize. At most he merely affirms the existence of The Way. . . . He stands at the vortex: When the philosophical, psychological, and scientific lines of thought are followed to the point where each becomes a cul-de-sac, as logic without faith eventually must, Dylan is there to sing his songs. Perhaps it is only at a time like ours that anyone will listen." Bob Dylan's self-appraisal is more terse and humble: "I just have thoughts in my head and I write them. I'm not trying to lead any causes for anyone."

In 1963 Dylan twice became the subject of controversy. The first incident occurred in the spring when he was scheduled to appear on the *Ed Sullivan Show* singing his "Talking John Birch Society Blues." The network regarded this number as too controversial and refused to permit its presentation (with Mr. Sullivan dissenting strongly). Dylan refused to appear on the program. In December of the same year he shocked the country when, as the recipient of the Tom Paine Award from the Emergency Civil Liberties Committee, he made a speech in which he expressed sympathy for Lee Harvey Oswald, the alleged assassin of President John F. Kennedy.

Another Side of Bob Dylan, an album released in 1964, became another of his best sellers. His recordings, appearances at concerts and at folk festivals, performances over television, recitals at colleges, European tours—all helped to make him a cult among devotees of folk music who favored his political thinking and recognized him as a performer, song-

writer, and poet of singular importance as a voice of his times. His success and wealth notwithstanding he changed little. He continued to favor rough clothes: denim jeans, a turtleneck shirt, worn-out jackets, and boots. He remained indifferent to the luxuries money could buy, never knew how much he was earning, and never seemed to care. He avoided accumulating possessions, or for that matter living in any one place for any length of time. His favorite mode of transportation was not a chauffeured limousine (which he now could well afford) but his motorcycle. The main change in his life came about through his marriage to Sarah Lownds, with whom he ultimately had five children, and for whom he acquired two brownstone houses in the Greenwich Village section of New York and a country place in Woodstock, New York. But not even marriage and parenthood could release him from his lifelong restlessness, loneliness, and introversion. The pressures of a successful career led him to indulge in drugs which he has since rejected. Since then he has reassessed his Jewish heritage and has become deeply involved in the study of Jewish history and literature.

By 1965 Dylan realized he had to seek out a new avenue of creativity; that singing about social injustices and other contemporary problems no longer stimulated him. He felt an all-compelling need to express himself, his inner being, his loneliness, his own place in society, his frustrations, his dreams. As he explained: "I want to write from inside me." In tapping such new personal themes, Dylan changed his style of songwriting. He began to favor a rock idiom which he skillfully blended into his former folk manner; he even began using an electrified guitar (the favorite of rock performers) in place of his acoustical one, as well as amplifiers. The new Dylan emerged in his number "Bringing It All Back Home," accompanied by electric instruments, (a record released in March of 1965). This was followed by "Mr. Tam-

Dylan

bourine Man," one of the best-selling records in seven countries, a song that made a star of The Byrds who recorded it with electric guitars and amplifiers. "Folkrock," as the new Dylan style was dubbed, became the subject of hot dispute. It was violently denounced by those who had idolized him for his folksongs or for his social viewpoints, or for both. At the Newport Festival in July 1965 former admirers expressed resentment at a performance of his new songs with a riot.

If he had lost one segment of his audience, he now gained a far greater one, among a young generation to whom rock represented a basic musical language. Dylan's album *Highway 61 Revisited,* released in August 1965, sold more copies than any previous Dylan album. This collection included such now accepted Dylan classics as "Like a Rolling Stone," "Ballad of a Thin Man," "Queen Jane Approximately," and "It Takes a Lot to Laugh." In this album, Steven Goldberg wrote, "his talent was rapidly achieving parity with his vision. He now felt more at home with that vision and was less obsessed with detailing its every aspect. This enabled him to return partially to the subject of man." Another group of personalized songs appeared in the album *Blonde on Blonde* in May of 1966. This included "Rainy Day Women, Nos. 12 and 35," "Pledging My Time," "Visions of Johanna," "Just Like a Woman," "Memphis Blues Again," and "Sad-Eyed Lady of the Lowlands." Of this collection Goldberg wrote: "Dylan's poetic talents are at their zenith. . . . Vision overwhelms him less than before, and he concentrates on finding peace through the kinds of women he had always loved; women of silent wisdom, women who are artists of life, women who neither argue nor judge, but accept the flow of things."

In replying to those who insisted he was "selling out" in order to reach a larger audience and gain a greater income and more formidable successes, Dy-

lan replied: "I can't sing 'With God on Our Side' for fifteen years. I was doing fine, you know, singing and playing my guitar. It was a sure thing, don't you understand, it was a sure thing. I was getting very bored with that. I couldn't go out and play like that. I was thinking of quitting."

The new Dylan became even more successful than the older one had been; even some of the admirers who had turned against him began returning to the Dylan fold. He was now at the height of his career when it suddenly seemed to come to a permanent end. Riding his motorcycle at top speed in 1966 he lost control and was almost killed. After an extended period of hospitalization, he went into total retirement with his wife and children. Except for a release of some of his early protest songs in an album called *Bob Dylan's Greatest Hits* he recorded nothing for eighteen months.

A new album came in 1968, *John Wesley Harding,* one of his greatest sellers. Here his songs revealed a new tranquillity and compassion, voiced a personal religion. "This album," wrote Mr. Goldberg, "is Dylan's supreme work; it is his solution to the seeming contradiction of vision and life." Mike Jahn reported in *High Fidelity*: "He hammers in several themes: I am simple; I am kind; I am lonely; I have been misunderstood; I am not my image." The cream of this crop included "Dear Landlord," "I Dreamed I Saw St. Augustine," "Drifter's Escape," "I Am a Lonesome Hobo," and "I'll Be Your Baby Tonight" (the last of which received the ASCAP Award in 1970 as one of the most frequently performed songs over a period of years). Even more personal and more passionately emotional were some of the songs in his next release, the album *Nashville Skyline,* which sold over one million copies in 1969. In this group are found "To Be Alone with You," "Lay Lady Lay," and "Tonight I'll Be Staying Here with You." *Self Portrait,* which followed in 1970, had an advance order totaling three million dollars and became Dylan's seventh (and second consecutive) gold record. In *Self Portrait,* for the first time since his first album, Dylan sang numbers written by others as well as a dozen of his own songs. He even included a popular song by Rodgers and Hart ("Blue Moon"). The critics, in general, found *Self Portrait* to be inferior Bob Dylan. "From being an avant-gardist," wrote Peter Schjeldahl in the New York *Times,* "he seems to have developed into a sort of American folk Meistersinger and minstrel. . . . Even the original songs have about them an air of having been resurrected."

New Morning, an album released in 1970, found Bob Dylan in top form. Here Dylan introduced twelve new songs, among which were the title number together with "If Dogs Run Free," "Time Passes Slowly," "Went to See the Gypsy," "Day of the Locusts," "Sign on the Window," and "If Not for You." The album ended with two religious inventions—one spoken like a sermon, the other ("Father of Night") described by critic Greil Marcus in the New York *Times* as a "ghostly Calvinistic rumble." Of the album as a whole, Greil Marcus said: "The riffs, inventions and studio jams . . . have their own personality . . . the full joy of anticipating the right move and the exhilaration of hitting it square and bouncing off a chord into a new lyric. . . . As the lines and phrases of *New Morning* pass into our speech, we may find that Bob Dylan's remarkable new songs not only speak to us, but give us the means by which we can, for a time, speak among ourselves." Said Mike Jahn, also in the New York *Times*: "*New Morning* is something of a lyrical return to the old poetic image; spiced as it is with odd messages and trails of thought."

In 1970 Bob Dylan received an honorary doctorate from Princeton University, an event that inspired him to write "Day of the Locusts," about a man incapable of adjusting himself to academic ceremonies. In 1971 he wrote and recorded a blues number, "Watching the River Flow."

In addition to resuming recording in 1968, Bob Dylan also returned to the concert stage where he began to command a fee of $50,000 for an appearance (against a percentage). In 1968 he appeared in Carnegie Hall at a memorial concert honoring Woody Guthrie and later that year he was heard in a joint concert with Johnny Cash, on whose television program he subsequently appeared as guest artist. Dylan has also sung in Europe. His concert on the Isle of Wight, off England, during the summer of 1969, attracted an audience of almost two hundred thousand rabid fans from all parts of Europe.

Bob Dylan was starred in a motion picture, *Don't Look Back* (1967), produced in England and acclaimed there as one of the best films of the year. He also contributed some songs to the motion picture *Little Fauss and Big Halsy,* in 1970. His first book, *Tarantula,* was published in 1971.

ABOUT:

Ewen, D. Great Men of American Popular Song; Kramer, D. Bob Dylan; Ribakove, S. and Ribakove, B. Folk Rock: The Bob Dylan Story; Scaduto, A. Bob Dylan: An Intimate Biography; Thompson, T. Positively Main Street.

New York Times, June 21, 1970; Reader's Digest, June 1970; Saturday Review, May 30, 1970.

Gus Edwards 1879-1945

See *Popular American Composers,* 1962.

Duke Ellington 1899-

For biographical sketch and list of earlier songs and compositions see *Popular American Composers,* 1962.

Among Ellington's most important compositions between 1960 and 1963 were *Thursday Suite,* for orchestra (based on John Steinbeck's *Sweet Thursday*), heard at Monterey Jazz Festival; jazz adaptations of Tchaikovsky's *Nutcracker Suite* and Grieg's *Peer Gynt Suite;* and *Afro-Bossa,* a musical examination of Afro-Iberian contributions to American music. He also contributed background music for a TV series, *Asphalt Jungle,* in 1962, from which came the song "I Want to Love You" (lyrics by Marshall Barer), based on the score's principal theme.

In 1963 Ellington opened a new avenue of performance and creativity for himself by presenting a "jazz-sacred" concert of his own works at the Grace Cathedral in San Francisco. This unconventional idea was first broached to him by Canon John Yaryan and Dean C. Julian Bartlett of the Grace Cathedral. Ellington was hesitant. "I was shocked," he later revealed to an interviewer. "How was I going to stand up in that big cathedral and make a noise?" Being a highly religious man and recognizing the opportunity such an event would provide him for writing reverent music, for preaching "musical sermons," for making "statements of eternal truths," Ellington finally agreed. At the service a choir sang music Ellington wrote for this occasion, its principal subject matter derived from the first four words of the Bible; this is the reason the composition is named *In the Beginning God.* A tap dancer performed before the altar. This performance proved so successful that Ellington and his performers appeared in numerous other houses of worship, including the Cathedral Church of St. John the Divine in New York, Coventry Cathedral in England, and in several synagogues (where Ellington's music was sung in Hebrew). For these events, Ellington created a repertory of religious music in jazz style. Among them were: *Supreme Being, Almighty God, Heaven, Too Good to Title, Something About Believing, Freedom,* and *Christmas Surprise.*

The year 1963 also saw him make his first foreign tour sponsored by the State Department. He and his orchestra were heard in the Middle East, India, Ceylon, Japan. Ellington wrote a number of works inspired by some of the places he visited on the tour: *The Far East Suite, Isfahan,* and *Mount Harissa.*

In the same year Ellington made a meaningful musical contribution to the betterment of racial relationships—*My People.* This ambitious score for a spectacular production was mounted at the Century of Negro Progress Exposition in Chicago between August 16 and September 12. Combining music and dance, it traced a century of Negro experience in America. It described the celebrated confrontation of Bull Connor and Martin Luther King at Birmingham, Alabama, and came to a climax with the song "What Color Is Virtue?" In addition to this work, Ellington completed in 1963 the background music for *Timon of Athens,* produced at the Shakespeare Festival Theater at Stratford, Ontario.

For his first appearance with his orchestra at the Lincoln Center for the Performing Arts in New York, during the summer of 1964, Ellington featured a new symphonic-jazz work: *Golden Broom and Green Apple.* Before 1964 ended, Ellington and six men of his orchestra returned to the Lincoln Center in the "Great Performers Series" where he introduced his *A Blue Mural from Two Perspectives.*

In 1965 Ellington wrote the background music for the motion picture *Assault on a Queen.* A good deal of controversy over Ellington was aroused in 1965 when he failed to receive a special citation from the Pulitzer Prize Committee for the "vitality and originality of his total productivity" even though he had been recommended for it by the three-man jury. In the ensuing storm, two members of the Pulitzer Prize committee (Winthrop Sargeant and Robert Eyer) resigned, while violent opposition to the final decision was voiced by several other members. But Ellington was not denied recognition that year. In August, Paul Screvane, city council president, awarded him the New York City Bronze Medal for his contributions to music. As for Ellington's own reaction to the Pulitzer Prize scandal, his comment was merely: "Fate is being kind to me. Fate doesn't want me to be famous too young."

In 1966 Ellington wrote the music for *Pousse Café,* an unsuccessful Broadway musical. As if in compensation, he was awarded a Grammy for the best large instrumental jazz performance that year. Ellington received a second Grammy in 1968 for *The Far East Suite,* as the year's best jazz recording.

The death of Ellington's friend and esteemed collaborator and orchestrator, Billy Strayhorn, in 1967 was a personal blow. But it did not stem the tide of Ellington's musical activity. He continued making numerous appearances both in America and abroad, most of the time with his own orchestra, sometimes as a guest conductor of major symphony orchestras in performances of his own music. In 1969 and 1970, Ellington completed an eleven-month tour of Europe, the Orient, Bangkok, New Zealand, and Australia. He returned to the United States to fill a five-week engagement at the Rainbow Grill in New York in August 1970 where he presented excerpts from one of his new works, *New Orleans Suite.* He had written this for the New Orleans Jazz Festival and played it in its entirety at a concert at Philharmonic Hall at the Lincoln Center for the Performing Arts on April 16, 1971. This was one of two major Ellington scores completed in 1970, the other being music for a ballet, *The River,* choreography by Alvin Ailey, presented by the American Ballet Theater at the Lincoln Center for the Performing Arts on June 25, 1970. The ballet was described by Clive Barnes of the New York *Times* as "marvelous . . . that rare thing among classic scores, something that is contemporary, moving and yet totally unsentimental." Ellington's score contains seven dances which the composer planned to expand into a major work consisting of prologue, eleven sections, and an epilogue.

In February 1970 Ellington was elected a member of the National Institute of Arts and Letters. On February 23 at Madison Square Garden in New York he received a monumental tribute. On the occasion of his seventieth birthday he was invited to the White House by President and Mrs. Richard M. Nixon. The President played "Happy Birthday" for Ellington on the piano, then presented him with the Presidential Medal of Freedom. "In the royalty of American music," said Mr. Nixon, "no man swings more or stands higher than the Duke."

Another tribute to Ellington on his seventieth birthday was the release of an album containing many all-time Ellington favorites, some Ellington compositions that had never been previously recorded, and seven new Ellington works. John S. Wilson reviewed the new works in the album in the New York *Times*: "Each [is] distinctively Ellingtonian except for the novel 'Fifi' which brings the Duke to a new instrument. '4:30 Blues' is a dark bit of swampy atmosphere hung with Spanish moss, carried on Russell Procoope's ripe, low-register clarinet. The Duke eases into 'Laying on Mellow' on the piano, building a casually rocking setting over which Hodges blows a blues full of exultant cries and sly runs. 'B. P.' is a solo run-through for Harold Ashby's tenor saxophone, while 'Tootie for Cootie' . . . is a showcase for Cootie Williams' bristling, rough-grained trumpet."

In 1969 Ellington wrote the background music for the motion picture *Change of Mind.* In 1970 his definitive biography was published, *The World of Duke Ellington* by Stanley Dance.

In 1971 Ellington received honorary Doctor of Music degrees from St. John's University, New York, and Berklee College of Music, Boston. The first American popular composer admitted to the Royal Swedish Academy, he was inducted March 12, 1971.

Emmett

Dan Emmett 1815-1904

See *Popular American Composers,* 1962.

Ludwig Englander 1859-1914

See *Popular American Composers,* 1962.

Sammy Fain 1902-

For biographical sketch and list of earlier songs see *Popular American Composers,* 1962.

———

"Tender Is the Night," the song Fain wrote to lyrics by Paul Francis Webster in 1961 as the title number for a motion picture, was nominated for an Academy Award in 1962, and became a best seller in a recording by Tony Bennett. In 1963 Fain contributed background music for the motion picture *The Incredible Mr. Limpet,* and the score for a stage musical, *Around the World in Eighty Days,* produced at the Marine Theater in Jones Beach, Long Island, during the summers of 1963 and 1964. In 1964 he wrote the title song for the motion picture *Joy in the Morning* (lyrics by Webster).

Fain made his return to the Broadway musical stage on November 10, 1964, with the unsuccessful production of *Something More,* starring Barbara Cook. The best songs (lyrics by Marilyn and Alan Bergman) were "Better All the Time," "I Feel Like New Year's Eve," and "In No Time at All."

Fred Fisher 1875-1942

See *Popular American Composers,* 1962.

George Forrest 1915-

and

Robert Wright 1914-

WHETHER writing for the screen, musical stage, or television, George "Chet"

GEORGE FORREST and
ROBERT WRIGHT

Fabian Bachrach

Forrest has always collaborated with Robert Wright. Their finest songwriting has been done for successful stage musicals in which they made popular adaptations of the music of serious composers of the past.

George Chichester Forrest, Jr., was born in Brooklyn, New York, on July 31, 1915, the son of a banker and investment counselor. He attended high schools in Florida, graduating from Palm Beach High School in 1931, and then studied music with Marion André in Fort Worth and with Fannie Greene in New York City. After the termination of his schooling, both academic and musical, he earned his living as a leader and pianist of dance orchestras, by playing the piano on cruise ships, accompanying popular performing artists, and entertaining in nightclubs.

In 1936 Forrest formed a collaboration arrangement with Robert Wright with whom he would henceforth write both the lyrics and the music for various media. Their first joint effort was a short motion picture feature produced by MGM—*New Shoes,* in 1936.

Robert Craig Wright was born on September 25, 1914, in Daytona Beach, Florida, the son of a commercial chemist.

Wright was graduated from Miami High School in 1931, immediately after which he wrote some special material for Helen Morgan who was then starring in a Miami hotel. From 1931 to 1933 he attended the University of Miami, a period in which he studied the piano with Mana Zucca and Olive Dungan. Like Forrest he then earned his livelihood as a dance-orchestra pianist, as accompanist, and as an organist in theaters.

After their first attempt at collaboration with *New Shoes* in 1936, Forrest and Wright went to Hollywood. For seven years, beginning with the motion picture *The Longest Night* in 1936, they were employed at the MGM studios writing lyrics, or lyrics and music, for songs placed in over two dozen major productions and numerous short features; occasionally they also did the scoring, or the writing, of background music. Among the important motion pictures in which they were involved during this period were *Sweethearts, The New Moon, Maytime, The Firefly, Music in My Heart,* and *I Married an Angel.* In 1940-1941 they were employed by Columbia, RKO, and United Artists in rapid succession; then they returned to the MGM lot.

Their most successful song of the years in Hollywood was "The Donkey Serenade" from the screen adaptation of Rudolf Friml's operetta *The Firefly.* "The Donkey Serenade" had not been in the original score. When the operetta was filmed, Forrest and Wright (aided by Herbert Stothart) took the melody of an early Friml piece for the piano (*Chanson*), which had subsequently been made by Sigmund Spaeth into the song "Chansonette." They adapted this material skillfully into an altogether new song, "The Donkey Serenade," which Allan Jones introduced in the motion picture musical and which later achieved an extraordinary sale with his recording. "The Donkey Serenade" became one of the major hit songs of 1937 (the year the film adaptation of *The Firefly* was released), was nominated for an Academy Award, and has since become a standard.

Without borrowed material, Forrest and Wright contributed to the screen the following songs worth noting: "Always and Always" to *Mannequin* (1937); the title number of *Saratoga* (1937); "At the Balalaika" to *Balalaika* (1939); "Morning Star" to *Dance, Girl, Dance* (1940); and "It's a Blue World" to *Music In My Heart* (1940).

While working for motion pictures, Forrest and Wright also contributed songs to major radio productions such as the *Vicks Radio Hour* in 1936, Maxwell House *Good News Hour* in 1937, and *Tune Up Time* in 1940, all three over the NBC network Later, in 1942 and 1943, they wrote songs for the United States Treasury radio programs and, in 1950, for *Startime Hour.*

While still in Hollywood, they also wrote scores for stage musicals in Los Angeles. One was *Thank You, Columbus,* produced at the Hollywood Playhouse on November 15, 1940. In 1941 they provided lyrics for additional music interpolated in stock company presentations of *Naughty Marietta* and *Rio Rita* produced in Los Angeles and San Francisco; and in August 1941 they wrote the score for *Fun for the Money* presented at the Hollywood Playhouse.

Their last screen score before leaving California in 1942 was the adaptation of the Rodgers and Hart musical *I Married an Angel.* During that summer Forrest and Wright worked at Camp Tamiment, an adult resort in the Pocono mountains in Pennsylvania. There they wrote the material for weekly revues. During the decade that followed, they wrote for various nightclub revues in New York and in Hollywood, California, and provided special material for major entertainers, including Jane Froman, Celeste Holm, and Robert Sterling.

Their initiation into the field of the Broadway musical came with the *Ziegfeld Follies of 1943,* a highly successful production for which they wrote some mate-

41

rial. This was followed by the first Broadway musical to which they contributed the complete score: *Song of Norway,* which opened on August 21, 1944, and had a run of 860 performances. The text was loosely based on the life of the Norwegian composer Edvard Grieg, with concentration on his earlier years and his romance with the singer Nina Hagerup, a childhood sweetheart he temporarily deserted for a prima donna. When his lifelong friend and inspiration, the poet-composer Rikard Nordraak, dies, Grieg marries his childhood sweetheart and goes on to fulfill his destiny as Norway's greatest composer.

The entire Forrest score was based on Grieg's music, tastefully and skillfully adapted into such outstanding popular musical numbers as "Strange Music" (based on *Wedding Day in Troldhaugen* from *Lyric Pieces* for the piano, and from *Nocturne*)—one of the principal song hits of the season of 1944-1945; "I Love You" (based on Grieg's own love song for Nina, "Ich liebe Dich"); "Freddy and His Fiddle" (derived from the *Norwegian Dance No. 2).*

Acclaimed by the critics, and a favorite with Broadway audiences, *Song of Norway* went on to become an operetta classic with numerous revivals throughout America for over a quarter of a century. Finally, in 1970, extensively revised, it was made into a lavish, colorful, and immensely successful motion picture. Filmed in Norway, it starred Edward G. Robinson, Florence Henderson, and Robert Morley, with a newcomer, Toralv Maurstad, playing the role of Grieg.

It was almost a decade before Forrest and Wright returned to Broadway with a musical as successful as *Song of Norway.* In the interim they directed and wrote new lyrics for an adaptation of Victor Herbert's *The Fortune Teller* and *Serenade* made into a single operetta and retitled *Gypsy Lady.* It came to New York on September 17, 1946; under the name of *Romany Love* it was produced in London in 1947. It was not a box office

success; nor was their adaptation of Heitor Villa-Lobos' music with their own lyrics, *Magdalena,* which opened in New York on September 20, 1948. In 1949 they wrote *The Great Waltz,* an operetta based on the life and music of Johann Strauss II. Produced first in Los Angeles, it subsequently toured the western United States and was produced with great success in London.

Their second Broadway stage triumph came with *Kismet,* on December 3, 1953. The composers tapped the rich vein of the music of Alexander Borodin to produce a "musical extravaganza" which the program described as a "musical Arabian night." Its setting was ancient Bagdad; its main character a young caliph who falls in love with and marries the daughter of the public poet. The score boasted two hits: "Stranger in Paradise" (melody based on the *Polovtsian Dances* from *Prince Igor*) and "And This Is My Beloved" (based on the main theme from the slow movement of the D major String Quartet). "Baubles, Bangles and Beads" and "Fate" were of subsidiary interest. *Kismet* remained on Broadway for almost 600 performances during which it won a Tony and an Outer Circle Award as the season's best musical. In 1955 it was made by MGM into a motion picture in an adaptation by Forrest and Wright. In 1971 a production of *Kismet* made a thirteen-week tour of the United States.

After *Kismet,* Forrest and Wright seemed to have lost their magic touch. In 1957 *The Carefree Heart* (for which they wrote the book based on the "Doctor" comedies of Molière, as well as the lyrics and music) opened and closed out of town; so did *At the Grand* in 1958. (Forrest and Wright prepared a revised version of *The Carefree Heart* for London in 1959, retitling the musical *Love Doctor,* but this version also failed.) *Kean,* a Broadway musical based on the life of the famous actor, had a run of less than a hundred performances after opening on November 2, 1961. Later in the 1960's, *Dumas, Father and Son* tried out in Los Angeles, was found wanting, and never came to New York, while *Anya* (whose songs came from the music of Rachmaninoff) had only a brief stay, on Broadway in 1965. They subsequently revised *Anya* and renamed it *I Live Again. Musical Theatre Cavalcade,* presented in Los Angeles in August of 1970, ran for just thirteen performances. In 1970 Forrest and Wright completed a musical comedy adaptation of Rostand's *Cyrano de Bergerac.*

Forrest and Wright share an apartment in Brooklyn, New York, and a winter home in Cocoanut Grove in Miami. They also have the same interests: travel, opera, concerts, and the theater.

ABOUT:
Ewen, D. New Complete Book of the American Musical Theater.

Stephen Foster 1826-1864

See *Popular American Composers,* 1962.

Anatole Friedland 1888-1938

See *Popular American Composers,* 1962.

Rudolf Friml 1879-

For biographical sketch and list of earlier songs see *Popular American Composers,* 1962.

———

Since 1962 (despite his advanced age) Friml has made many public appearances in America and Europe as pianist in programs devoted entirely to his own music. His ninetieth birthday was saluted by ASCAP in New York on December 7, 1969. With Friml present, songs from his most famous operettas were sung. Ogden Nash contributed a set of witty verses in a tribute ending with the lines: "I trust that your conclusion and mine are similar; 'Twould be a

happier world if it were Frimler." At the end of these festivities, a triple-tiered birthday cake, blazing with candles, was wheeled up to the stage. Friml, his wife, and the actor Dennis King joined in blowing out the candles.

A Rudolf Friml Library was established at the University of California in Los Angeles in 1970 comprising a hundred original manuscripts as well as tapes and recordings.

Percy Gaunt 1852-1896

See *Popular American Composers,* 1962.

Bobbie Gentry 1942-

BOBBIE GENTRY was born Bobbie Street on a farm in Chickasaw, Mississippi, on July 27, 1942. Her parents were divorced when she was a year old, and during the next six years she was raised by her grandparents in her own home. When Bobbie was six, her grandmother traded in a cow for a piano. Hardly had the instrument entered the home when Bobbie began learning to play it.

Soon after her sixth year, Bobbie's family moved to Greenwood, in the Mississippi delta country. There she attended grade school and, when she was seven, wrote her first song, "My Dog Sergeant Is a Good Dog." Here, too, she had her first experience sleeping in a feather bed, which she later recalled in her song "Hurry, Tuesday Child."

In her thirteenth year, Bobby Gentry moved to Arcadia, California, to join her mother who had remarried. Two years later the family moved to Palm Springs. Now fifteen, Bobbie was writing songs continually, and performing them in fashionable clubs where Hoagy Carmichael, Bob Hope, Phil Harris, and other celebrities heard and encouraged her. It was at this time that she changed her surname to Gentry (after seeing the motion picture *Ruby Gentry).*

Gentry

BOBBIE GENTRY

For a time she attended the University of California at Los Angeles and the Los Angeles Conservatory of Music where she studied the guitar. She supported herself by doing secretarial work and by performing at small nightspots on weekends. She also wrote and arranged little revues. All the while she continued studying music by herself, perfecting her skill on the guitar and learning to play the piano, banjo, vibes, and bass as well. Her progress as a performer tempted her to abandon both her formal schooling and her work as secretary, since she could now command $450 a week as the leader of a singing and dancing group.

Songwriting became her major interest in 1967 (she always wrote the words to her melodies). In that year she made a demonstration record of one of her numbers, "Mississippi Delta," sung to her own guitar accompaniment. A friend brought it to a producer at Capitol Records who signed Miss Gentry to a contract both as singer and as composer.

Late one night in 1967, following a singing engagement, she felt the creative urge. Browsing through a notebook which she used to jot down various thoughts, ideas, and little experiences, she came upon the following line: "Billy Joe McCallister jumped off the Tallahatchie Bridge." This sparked a song idea. The following morning she completed a seven-minute ballad which made song history, "Ode to Billy Joe." "I wrote it like a story, almost like a play," she has explained. There is an air of mystery to the subject matter of the lyric in which a preacher, Brother Taylor, sees Billy Joe and his girl throw something off the bridge with no explanation as to precisely what it was.

She recorded it herself for Capitol. Released in 1967, it reached the top of the best-seller list in four weeks. Eventually it sold over four million disks in recordings by some sixty performers other than Miss Gentry. Her recording received three Grammys as the best female vocal performance, the best female solo vocal recording, and the year's best new artist.

To Bobbie Gentry, the theme of "Ode to Billy Joe" is "indifference." She explains :"I'm not a protest singer. I merely pour out human nature. . . . But you don't have to be from the South to get the message."

To Leonard Feather, "Miss Gentry's legend achieves an exquisite irony as parents and daughter sit around the dinner table discussing the tragedy, interpreting their reactions with such side comments as 'pass the biscuits, please,' and 'I'll have another piece of apple pie.'" Miss Gentry commented: "They could have been passing around ravioli or bagels. In the song I wanted to show people's lack of ability to relate to someone else's tragedy."

A single song, and a single recording, made Bobbie Gentry a celebrity. She began to appear as guest artist on major television programs following her TV debut on the Johnny Carson Show. She was one of the few Americans invited to compete at the famous San Remo Song Festival in Italy where her performance of "La Siepa" brought her the Italian Press Award.

Two years after "Ode to Billy Joe" came another million-disk record seller for Bobbie Gentry, the song "Fancy," for which she once again wrote words and music, and which she herself recorded. In this number, released in November of 1969, Miss Gentry propounds the thesis that each day is the first one of the rest of our lives, that we must make it count, no matter what choices we make. "Fancy" received the ASCAP Country Music Award in 1970.

Bobbie Gentry has produced a repertory of songs, most of which have a pronounced Southern flavor; she is particularly adept in writing blues indigenous to the delta region of Mississippi. Some of her songs have strong characterizations, almost as if the characters in the lyrics stepped out of the pages of William Faulkner. As Harvey Geller wrote: "The strength of her music is believability. It is an outpouring of authenticity."

These are among her best songs: "Poppa Won'tcha Let Me Go to Town with You," "I Saw an Angel Die," "Oklahoma River Bottom Band," "Penduli Pendulum," "Louisiana Man," "Courtyard," "Hushabye Mountain," "Sweet Peony," "Less of Me," "Mornin' Glory" (words by Glen Campbell), "Touch 'Em with Love," "Casket Vignette," "Chickasaw," "Country Girl," "Seasons Come, Seasons Go," "Big Boss Man," and "All I Have to Do Is Dream."

The year 1969 was particularly eventful for Miss Gentry. She achieved first place in England's listing of best-selling records with her recording of Bacharach's "I'll Never Fall in Love Again." She filmed fourteen TV specials for the BBC, besides making numerous guest appearances on other English TV productions. In Holland she appeared at the Dutch Grand Gala. For Capitol Records she wrote an album of Christmas songs, *Christmas Picture Book*. She was starred in several major American TV specials and made numerous personal appearances in leading nightclubs and hotels.

She also did thirteen programs for the Armed Forces Radio and TV Services entitled "The Bobbie Gentry Show."

Her wealth enabled her to acquire a twenty-five-room Spanish-type villa on a two-acre wooded property near Beverly Hills in California. She resides there with her housekeeper, two red-tailed sharks, and her dog, Yorkie. On December 18, 1969, she married William Harrah, the fifty-eight-year-old wealthy Nevada casino operator. But following their honeymoon in Europe, they separated; in April 1970 they were divorced. She has since resumed her career with outstanding success; for example, five performances in Portland, Oregon, in November of 1970 attracted an audience of 80,000 and brought box office receipts exceeding $150,000.

In 1971 she recorded the album *Patchwork* which included several ballads such as "Jeremiah," "Beverly," and "Marigolds and Tangerines" and the country blues "Billy the Kid" and "Mean Stepmama Blues."

Miss Gentry is attractive and glamorous: tall, slim, radiating sex appeal. She wears her dark auburn (formerly black) hair in an upsweep over a face glowing with electric brown eyes and an infectious smile. She speaks as she sings, in a raspy Southern drawl. *Hi-Fi Stereo* said: "She is able to project sex, sincerity, and an unmorbid-sadness through her voice; and . . . she possesses the relaxed assurance of a true professional. . . . She is the first singer, to my knowledge, who has made a 'delta blues' truly popular and since it is a legitimate, authentic and rich current in American music, she has . . . an extraordinary mine of material to work. How sensitively and perceptively she works with it is readily apparent."

ABOUT:

Roxon, L. Rock Encyclopedia; Stambler, I. and Landon, G. Encyclopedia of Folk, Country, and Western Music.

Gershwin

George Gershwin 1898-1937

For biographical sketch and list of songs see *Popular American Composers,* 1962.

———

George Gershwin's posthumous fame, which had been developing so prodigiously since his death in 1937, increased after 1962.

A "George Gershwin Day" was proclaimed in New York City on September 26, 1963, and a commemorative plaque was affixed on the site of Gershwin's birthplace in Brooklyn, New York. In 1966 an elementary school in a black section of Chicago was dedicated as the George Gershwin School. A year later Gershwin became the first American composer to have a street in Europe named after him: George Gershwin Avenue in Hull, England.

In 1968 Mayor Lindsay of New York proclaimed the week of May 5 "George Gershwin Week" in conjunction with a retrospective exhibit of Gershwiniana entitled "Gershwin: George, the Music; Ira, the Words" at the Museum of Modern Art. In May 1968 a three-night Gershwin festival was held in Venice. Morton Gould conducted some of Gershwin's serious works, while four jazz groups offered the composer's popular tunes.

George Gershwin College was opened as a dormitory of the State University of New York at Stony Brook, Long Island, in 1969. The building houses a small theater, the George Gershwin Music Box. In the spring of 1970 the official dedication of the Music Box took place. The events included an exhibition of Gershwiniana (manuscripts, sheet music, first editions, photographs); excerpts in concert version from *Porgy and Bess;* and film presentations of *Porgy and Bess, Rhapsody in Blue,* and *An American in Paris.*

On October 27, 28, and 29, 1970 there took place in Miami, Florida, the world's first festival presenting all of Gershwin's serious works. Conceived and planned by the editor of this book and promoted by the School of Music of the University of Miami, the festival was under the artistic direction of Dr. Frederick Fennell, who conducted all three nights. The entire event was taped by the Voice of America and transmitted early in 1971 throughout the world (outside the United States) over a network of three thousand stations to an estimated audience of forty-five million; comments, introductions, and a half-hour interview with the editor of this book were translated into thirty-five languages.

During the decade 1960-1970, *Porgy and Bess*—the first opera by an American to do so—entered the permanent repertory of major European opera houses: first at the Volksoper in Vienna; subsequently at houses in Turkey, Bulgaria, France (six cities); the Komische Oper in East Berlin (presented in German); and the Copenhagen Opera (in Danish). In June 1970 *Porgy and Bess* was produced for the first time in Charleston, South Carolina, the city which serves as the setting of the text. This event, commemorating the three-hundredth anniversary of the founding of the city, made social history. It was the first time in the history of Charleston that the audience was not segregated, not only at the performance itself but also at a gala party that followed. During the summer of 1971 *Porgy and Bess* was produced at the Bergenz Festival in Austria.

Two Gershwin musicals were revived during the 1960's, one in New York, the other in London. *Lady, Be Good* was produced in London on July 25, 1968, and *Of Thee I Sing!* was revived Off Broadway on March 7, 1969. This was the first revival in New York since 1952, but since then *Of Thee I Sing* has been extensively performed in cities throughout the United States, particularly during the election years of 1964 and 1968. A third Gershwin musical, *Girl Crazy,* was made into a motion picture for the third time. Renamed *The Boys Meet the Girls,* and starring Connie Francis and Harve Presnell, it was released in 1965.

The biography of Gershwin by the

editor of this book, published in 1956 under the title *A Journey to Greatness: The Life and Music of George Gershwin*, was completely rewritten as well as updated and expanded and was published in 1970 under the title *George Gershwin: His Journey to Greatness*.

Other Gershwin events during the latter part of the 1960's included a one-hour documentary televised in England by the BBC; another documentary, prepared by a French company and televised in France; and a BBC radio program of Gershwin music lasting an hour and a half, broadcast throughout Europe.

On February 8, 1971, *Do It Again* began a short run in New York. This was a panorama of fifty-three Gershwin songs sung by Margaret Whiting and staged by Bert Conry. In the same year *Hey Dad Who Is This Guy Gershwin, Anyway?*, a new multimedia rock musical made up of Gershwin songs, produced and directed by Herb Hendler, appeared in Boston.

Ernest Gold 1921-

ERNEST GOLD, a prolific and successful composer of screen music, was born Ernest Siegmund Goldner in Vienna on July 13, 1921. He came from a family of musicians. His maternal grandfather, Dr. Sigmund Stransky, an industrialist, had studied with Anton Bruckner. Ernest's paternal grandfather, Moritz Goldner (a civil servant), was a graduate of the Vienna Conservatory who played the piano with professional skill and composed light music. Ernest's father, a lawyer, was an amateur violinist who studied with one of Vienna's most popular operetta composers, Richard Heuberger.

Ernest began to study the violin when he was six. Two years later he supplemented these lessons with instruction on the piano. Even in childhood he proved creative, piecing together little compositions at the piano which his father wrote down for him. Planning a professional career in music, he enrolled at the Acad-

ERNEST GOLD

emy of Music and Performing Arts when he was in his late teens. The invasion of Austria by Nazi Germany in 1938 made it impossible for him to complete his studies there. Ernest's mother had died five years earlier, and the remaining family—the father, Ernest, and Ernest's sister —fled to the United States, leaving behind all their possessions. When they arrived they had only thirty dollars.

Ernest's first job in the United States (as a busboy at the World's Fair in New York) lasted one day; he was fired for incompetence. His next position, more suitable to his talent, was as a piano accompanist at the Little Red Schoolhouse, a progressive school in New York; his salary was five dollars a week. This job, however, made few demands on his time, allowing him to devote himself to advancing the career which he had by now chosen: writing popular songs.

Shortly after it was formed, Broadcast Music, Inc. (BMI), hired Gold to write songs at a weekly salary of fifteen dollars. Of about forty songs he would write, the first to be published was "Here in the Velvet Night" (lyrics by Don McCray) in 1940. It was not noticed. Success, however, was not slow in coming. "Practice Makes Perfect" (lyrics by Don

47

Roberts) was popularized by Billie Holiday and also by Bob Chester. It was represented on radio's *Hit Parade* for seventeen weeks—four of those weeks occupying the number one spot. "Accidentally on Purpose" (Don McCray), made famous by Jack Teagarden, appeared on the *Hit Parade* for four weeks. Other songs of this early period in Gold's career were "Come Down to Earth, My Angel" (Robert Sour and Don McCray), introduced by "Fats" Waller; "Montevideo" (Sour and McCray), popularized by Harry James; and "They Started Something" (Sour and McCray), a Kate Smith favorite.

While writing songs for BMI, Gold studied dance arrangements and harmony with Otto Cesana, under whose guidance he wrote his first major orchestral composition. It was the *Pan American Symphony*, given two performances over the NBC network by the NBC Symphony under Frank Black.

Dissatisfied with the limited scope of his activity at BMI, Gold left his job to devote himself to further study, mainly of conducting, with Leon Barzin. He earned his living teaching composition privately, while continuing his own efforts as a serious composer. Gold's piano concerto was performed by Marisa Regules and the National Orchestral Association under Leon Barzin.

By this time, Gold had decided to try his luck as a composer for motion pictures. Screen music had always interested him. As a teenager he had followed with fascination the careers of Max Steiner and other successful Hollywood composers. Convinced now that he wanted to follow in Steiner's footsteps, Gold left New York for Hollywood. Ten days after he reached Los Angeles, he was given an assignment to write music for the first movie directed by Mel Ferrer—*The Girl of the Limberlost* (1945) based on Gene Stratton Porter's novel.

During the next few years, Gold worked for Republic Pictures where, as he puts it, "I learned my trade by providing music for numerous motion pictures. I was only a contributor to those scores, as it was then the practice to have perhaps three composers share the work (each getting a copy of the main themes to be used for some measure of coherence). That way a complete score could be turned out in a week or ten days. I never kept any of the pieces for those movies, nor remember their titles." Between 1946 and 1952 Gold was engaged to write the background music for a dozen other motion pictures, for four cartoons, and for one documentary.

A temporary hiatus in Gold's Hollywood career came in 1954 when he returned to New York and worked as rehearsal pianist for the Broadway musical *Plain and Fancy*. Back again in Hollywood, Gold contributed background music for *Affair in Havana, Man on the Prowl, Tarzan's Fight for Life, The Screaming Skull, Wink of an Eye,* and *Battle of the Coral Sea,* between 1957 and 1959.

In 1958 Stanley Kramer, the producer, needed five minutes of rock 'n' roll music for the film *The Defiant Ones*—a minor assignment which Gold took in stride but for which he was given the Laurel Award. In the same year, George Antheil, who for a decade had been exerting a powerful influence on Gold's technical development as a composer, died. Antheil, a distinguished composer who wrote for the movies, had been under contract to write the score for *On the Beach,* which Stanley Kramer was producing. When Antheil died, Kramer remembered Gold's work on *The Defiant Ones* and turned over Antheil's assignment to him. Gold's excellent score received an Academy Award, the Golden Globe Award of the Hollywood Foreign Press Association, and the *Downbeat* Award as the year's best dramatic score. Also in 1958, Gold wrote all the background music for *The Young Philadelphians*.

In 1960 Gold established his prominence in motion picture music with the most ambitious and important assignment he had yet received: writing the background music for *Exodus*, the movie based on Leon Uris's novel about the struggle for and the birth of Israel. With this score, Gold achieved the greatest success he had yet known: an Academy Award, and two Grammy awards—one for the best soundtrack album, and the other for the year's best song. That song, "The Exodus Song" (sometimes also known as "This Land Is Mine") had lyrics by Pat Boone, with a melody from the main theme of the score. Pat Boone's recording was a best seller; so was one performed by the two-piano team of Ferrante and Teicher.

In 1958 Gold had been appointed as musical director of the Santa Barbara Symphony, which he developed from an amateur group of thirty-five musicians into a well-developed symphony orchestra of over seventy men. Following his success with *Exodus*, Gold left the Santa Barbara Symphony. In 1964 he agreed, at the request of Mayor Yorty of Los Angeles, to form and conduct an orchestra made up entirely of senior citizens.

Since *Exodus*, Gold's most important music for the screen includes scores for such major productions as *Judgment at Nuremberg, A Child Is Waiting, It's a Mad, Mad, Mad, Mad World, Ship of Fools,* and *The Secret of Santa Vittoria.* He was nominated for Academy Awards for both *It's a Mad, Mad, Mad, Mad World* and *The Secret of Santa Vittoria.* Themes from some of his scores were transformed into popular songs, notably "On the Beach" (lyrics by Steven Allers) and "The Song of Santa Vittoria," also known as "Stay" (lyrics by Norman Gimbel), the latter made popular by Sergio Franchi.

Gold has written articles on music for the screen for numerous journals. In one of these he said: "Background music for the movies . . . is not unlike a plant growing on rocky cliff. The smallest crevice, the minutest quantity of soil is used by the plant to root itself. Similarly in motion picture music the tiny silences between lines, the brief moment needed for a reaction, the almost imperceptible hesitation before a bit of business—those are the crevices on the soundtrack which a composer must utilize to anchor his music."

Gold was married twice, the first time in 1943 to a Swiss painter, Andrée Golbin, whom he divorced five years later. In 1950 he married the American singer Marni Nixon, a marriage that lasted nineteen years and brought three children. Gold's principal hobby is horseback riding. He is a member of the California Dressage Society and owns a show horse named Frechdachs. Gold has served as president of the West Coast branch of the National Association for American Composers and Conductors. He has also devoted himself to lecturing, creating music for education, and has pursued his career as a serious composer. He believes that "an artist cannot write relevant motion picture music today unless he is involved in the many other forms of music making outside the motion picture field."

ABOUT:
ASCAP Biographical Dictionary (1966).

Edwin Franko Goldman
1878-1956

See *Popular American Composers,* 1962.

Jay Gorney 1896-

See *Popular American Composers,* 1962.

Morton Gould 1913-

For biographical sketch and list of earlier songs and compositions see *Popular American Composers,* 1962.

In 1964-1965 Gould contributed background music for a television documentary, *World War I,* a half-hour program series that ran twenty-six weeks, used footage from World War I news films, and was narrated by Robert Ryan. In 1967 Larry Adler and the Morton Gould orchestra recorded Gould's "Love for Two" (written for the wedding of Gould's oldest son, Eric), and "Night Walk" (composed expressly for Larry Adler). Morton Gould conducted several of Gershwin's concert works during a three-night Gershwin festival held in Venice, in May 1968.

John (Johnny) Green 1908-

For biographical sketch and list of earlier songs see *American Popular Composers,* 1962.

———

In 1961 Green was one of four Academy Award winners for the scoring of the motion picture *West Side Story.* He also served as the conductor and music codirector of this distinguished and preeminently successful screen production. In 1969 he once again received an Academy Award (this time without sharing the honor) for his scoring of *Oliver!* He was twice nominated for Oscars, in 1963 for the scoring of *Bye Bye Birdie,* and in 1970 for the scoring (in collaboration with Albert Woodbury) of *They Shoot Horses, Don't They?* The latter score included seven of Green's own song classics of the past, together with other standards of the 1920's and early 1930's.

Since 1962 Green has made numerous appearances as guest conductor of many of America's major symphony orchestras in programs of semiclassical and serious music. Between 1966 and 1968 he was on the State Committee of Public Education, to which he had been appointed by the governor of California. Since 1966 he has served as president of the Screen Composers Association of the United States, and has been a member of the Board of Governors of the Performing Arts Council of the Los Angeles Music Center.

Ferde Grofé 1892-1972

See *Popular American Composers,* 1962.

David W. Guion 1892-

See *Popular American Composers,* 1962.

Albert Hague 1926-

For biographical sketch and list of earlier songs see *Popular American Composers,* 1962.

———

To a libretto and lyrics by Allen Sherman, Hague provided the music for *Fig Leaves Are Falling,* an unsuccessful Broadway musical that opened in January of 1969.

W. C. Handy 1873-1958

For biographical sketch and list of earlier songs see *Popular American Composers,* 1962.

———

In 1969, in conjunction with the sesquicentennial celebration of the founding of the city of Memphis, Tennessee, a six-cent stamp was issued bearing Handy's likeness.

Ben Harney 1872-1938

See *Popular American Composers,* 1962.

Charles K. Harris 1867-1930

See *Popular American Composers,* 1962.

Will S. Hays 1837-1907

See *Popular American Composers,* 1962.

Ray Henderson 1896-1970

For biographical sketch and list of songs see *Popular American Composers,* 1962.

Ray Henderson died of a heart attack in Greenwich, Connecticut, on December 31, 1970.

Victor Herbert 1859-1924

See *Popular American Composers,* 1962.

Jerry Herman 1933-

JERRY HERMAN was born in New York City on July 10, 1933. His father owned a children's summer camp; his mother was a professional musican who taught voice and piano. During Jerry's childhood his family moved to Jersey City, New Jersey, where Jerry, at the age of six, began playing the piano by ear, in time acquiring considerable skill without the benefit of a lesson. Following his graduation from Henry Snyder High School in Jersey City, he enrolled at the Parsons School of Design in New York intending to become an interior decorator. While there he wrote his first song which he sold for two hundred dollars. From then on, songwriting was a major hobby until it ultimately became a profession.

Herman left the Parsons School of Design and abandoned his ambition to become an interior decorator in order to attend the University of Miami at Coral Gables, Florida. There he majored in drama and became involved in the school's stage productions. He inaugurated a varsity show, won a prize for playwriting, and contributed to the University paper. Partly because of his varied extracurricular activities he was elected to the school's principal honor society and listed in *Who's Who in American Colleges.*

JERRY HERMAN

In 1954 Herman graduated from the University of Miami with a degree of Bachelor of Arts. Convinced that he should be a writer he went to New York. In a short time he contributed special material for some major television stars, including Jane Froman, Garry Moore, and Ray Bolger, while supporting himself by playing the piano in a nightclub.

He made his theatrical debut in 1954 with an Off-Broadway production of a little musical, *I Feel Wonderful,* which had originally been produced at the University of Miami. Not only did he write the text, lyrics, and music for this show, but he also served as its producer and director. William Hawkins of the New York *World-Telegram and Sun* wrote: "It is safe to say that this twenty-two-year-old will be heard from in the future. He has a genuine comic feel and can turn out a song that is gay and hummable."

In 1958 a revue for which he wrote the songs was seen at a nightclub where Herman was the pianist. Two years later his second Off-Broadway musical, *Parade,* was produced but made little impression.

In 1961 Herman and a young playwright, Don Appel, discussed the possibility of writing a show with Israel as its setting. Receiving financial backing from Gerard Oestreicher, who was impressed with Herman's work, Herman and Appel did five weeks of intensive research in Israel with the cooperation of the Israeli government. Their musical, *Milk and Honey,* opened in New York on October 10, 1961, with a cast headed by Mimi Benzell, Robert Weede, and Molly Picon. While the book centered on the experiences of American tourists in Israel and involved the romance of a middle-aged American widow and an unhappily married American businessman, the chief interest lay in the way the production captured the spirit of the young country. Local color was vividly provided through Israeli ceremonies (including a Yemenite wedding and the celebration of independence day) and indigenous dances. The musical proved a success, lasting over a year on Broadway. Two of its songs—the title number and "Shalom"—became hits. Herman received a Tony Award as the best composer and lyricist of the year.

Madame Aphrodite, lyrics and music by Herman to a book by Tad Mosel based on his own television play, was a box office disaster when produced in 1961, lasting only thirteen performances. Herman rebounded from this failure with one of the greatest triumphs in theater history—*Hello, Dolly!,* based on Thornton Wilder's *The Matchmaker.* With Carol Channing as Dolly the matchmaker, and with Gower Champion's brilliant direction and choreography, *Hello, Dolly!* opened on Broadway on January 16, 1964. In its first year it grossed over four million dollars, playing continually to capacity houses and capturing no less than ten Tony awards (including one for Jerry Herman as best composer and lyricist), the New York Drama Critics Circle Award, and first place for Herman as composer and critic in a poll conducted by *Variety.* The original-cast recording was a best seller.

Though in the mold of old-fashioned musical comedies—in which the main function of the text was to provide a vehicle for the songs, production numbers, witty dialogue, and exciting dances —*Hello, Dolly!* earned the enthusiastic praise of the critics. "It will be an enormous success," prophesied Richard Watts, Jr. To Howard Taubman of the New York *Times* the production possessed "qualities of freshness that are rare in the run of our machine-made musicals. It transmutes the broadly stylized mood of the mettlesome farce into the gusto and colors of the musical stage." Once again Herman was selected as the composer-lyricist of the year, this time by a poll of the New York critics.

Hello, Dolly! made stage history on several counts. By the time it closed on December 27, 1970, it had accumulated the greatest number of performances—2,844—of any musical in Broadway history up to that time. During its Broadway run of six years and eleven months, six stars appeared as Dolly—Carol Channing (who originated the role), Ginger Rogers, Martha Raye, Betty Grable, Phyllis Diller, and Ethel Merman (with whom the show closed). When Ethel Merman took over the role in March of 1970 she brought down the house. For Miss Merman, Jerry Herman interpolated two new numbers into the production, "World, Take Me Back" and "Love, Look in My Window." (They had been in the score when it was first written and when Ethel Merman was being considered for the role Carol Channing assumed.) National companies, with some of the above-named stars in the title role, established box office records in city after city.

Hello, Dolly! became the only musical in the recent history of Broadway to have two productions running simultaneously on Broadway; the second one, made up of an all-Negro cast headed by Pearl Bailey, was first presented in 1967. The musical also became one of the most highly esteemed and lavish screen productions, with Barbra Streisand taking over the leading part, and Herman contributing two new songs as well as the scoring. Herman himself regards this motion picture as "the definitive statement" of this musical, adding that "in years to come the motion picture version will be the one that everybody will remember."

Finally, *Hello, Dolly!* gave American popular music one of the big hit songs of the decade—the title number. Herman had no idea he was writing anything more than a functional piece of music for a production number in the show when he wrote this song. It took him an afternoon to write a stylized number in the spirit of Lillian Russell and the 1890's. Then the unexpected happened. Louis Armstrong recorded it, and the song became an overnight sensation. "I went to a cast party where they had the first cut of the recording," Herman recalls. "Before that I never expected it would have any popular market, but the way the other members of the company loved it, I began to realize that it was going to be something special." It was. Louis Armstrong's record version sold well over a million disks. The song was recorded in seventy-two other versions in America and in thirty-five versions in Europe. The sheet music sold several hundred thousand copies. During the presidential campaign of 1964, Barry Goldwater's forces tried to adopt a parody as a campaign song (renamed "Hello, Barry!"), but were denied permission by the producer who opposed Mr. Goldwater's ideology. As "Hello, Lyndon," it was taken over by the Democratic party and introduced at the national convention in Atlantic City, with Jerry Herman at the piano.

So popular a hit as the title number inevitably overshadowed some of the other excellent songs of the score. Among them were "Before the Parade Passes," "Put On Your Sunday Clothes," "So Long, Dearie," and "Ribbons Down My Back."

Jerry Herman enjoyed another great success with *Mame,* a stage musical based on Patrick Dennis's popular novel which had been dramatized as *Auntie Mame* by Jerome Lawrence and Robert E. Lee. As a musical, *Mame* came to the Winter Garden on May 24, 1966, where it remained for over fifteen hundred performances. It received a Tony award as the year's best musical and a Grammy as the best score of an original-cast album. In this musical the main point of interest is the eccentric, uninhibited, and boisterous heroine (magnificently portrayed by Angela Lansbury), her successes and failures, her strange ideas on how to raise an orphaned nephew living with her, and her equally peculiar concept of how life should be lived. The play carries her through the years 1928 to 1946 and ends with her taking a trip around the world with her nephew's son. And in the finale the audience is told: "And so, if you read tomorrow that a glamorous American widow won a race on a mad water ox, then went on to a party for the Egyptian ambassador where she served cheese blintzes, it will be Mame."

Above and beyond the characterization of the heroine, this musical boasted some fine satirical episodes (including a takeoff on the kind of production numbers Broadway was partial to in the 1930's, and a mocking picture of Southern chivalry) and a rousing cakewalk that ends the first act. As in *Hello, Dolly!* the principal song was the title number in a score that had two other effective tunes in "My Best Girl" and "If He Walked into My Life." The latter received a Grammy in Eydie Gormé's recording as the best female vocal recording of the year.

Herman's attempt to make a musical out of Jean Giraudoux's *The Madwoman of Chaillot,* which followed, missed fire. It was called *Dear World* and lasted only a few weeks after opening on February 6, 1969. Here Herman's best musical numbers were "I Don't

Want to Know," "Each Tomorrow Morning," "Kiss Her Now," and the title number.

Discussing his work as composer and lyricist, Herman told an interviewer: "I believe in musical simplicity. I'm a tremendous Irving Berlin fan for that reason. I believe that when someone pays fifteen dollars to go to a musical, he deserves to be able to hum something on the way out. I'm a tremendous Richard Rodgers and Alan Jay Lerner and Frank Loesser fan, too."

Some of Herman's best melodies come to him as he walks the streets of New York. He concentrates so fiercely on musical ideas as he walks that he is convinced that some day he will be the victim of a passing vehicle. In developing his songs he works on both lyrics and music at the same time, fitting them together, he says, "like pieces in a jigsaw puzzle."

Herman lives in a four-room garden apartment on West Tenth Street in New York where, when he is not working, he spends his time reading and painting. He is comparatively short (five-foot-five) and slight (135 pounds), and looks much younger than he is. He maintains a summer home at Fire Island Pines where he can indulge in his favorite outdoor sport, swimming.

ABOUT:
Ewen, D. New Complete Book of the American Musical Theater.

John Hill Hewitt 1801-1890

See *Popular American Composers*, 1962.

Billy Hill 1899-1940

See *Popular American Composers*, 1962.

Louis Hirsch 1887-1924

See *Popular American Composers*, 1962.

Karl Hoschna 1877-1911

See *Popular American Composers*, 1962.

Joseph E. Howard 1867-1961

See *Popular American Composers*, 1962.

Raymond Hubbell 1879-1954

See *Popular American Composers*, 1962.

Victor Jacobi 1883-1921

See *Popular American Composers*, 1962.

Isham Jones 1894-1956

See *Popular American Composers*, 1962.

Scott Joplin 1868-1919

See *Popular American Composers*, 1962.

John Kander 1927-

JOHN KANDER was born in Kansas City, Missouri, on March 18, 1927. Although there was no background of music in the immediate family, when John was four, he began playing the piano. An aunt, noticing his interest, started to teach him chords, an experience he never forgot, for it opened up the rich tonal possibilities of piano music. His first piano lessons began when he was six and he made outstanding progress. He was ten when he saw his first opera, *Aida*, presented by the San Carlo Opera. "This was perhaps the most exciting event of my boyhood years," he recalls. "From that day on, I became an opera 'nut.' "

As a freshman at Westport High School Kander became the pupil of Wiktor Labunski, the piano teacher who exerted the first major influence in his musical development and with whom he

JOHN KANDER

remained as student through his high school years. "I always had a wonderful time with music," says Kander. "I was always thinking about it. It gave me my greatest pleasure." For his senior year at high school, he transferred to Pembroke Country Day School from which he was graduated and for which he wrote the school song.

After graduating from Pembroke Kander enrolled in Oberlin College because he wanted to combine an academic education with musical training at its Conservatory. He wrote the music for two productions at Oberlin, *Second Square Opus Two* and *Requiem for George,* with lyrics by James Goldman, a young student at the University of Chicago. Kander had met James, and James's brother, William, while all three attended a summer camp in 1937.

In 1951 Kander was graduated from Oberlin College. Aware that he wanted to become a professional musician, he joined the Goldman brothers, who wanted to be writers, in coming to New York where Kander received his Master of Arts degree at Columbia University. At Columbia Kander studied music with Jack Beeson, Otto Luening, and Douglas Moore. Moore became not only a

good friend but also the one to advise Kander about the direction his musical ambitions should take. At this time Kander aspired to be a serious composer, having produced a good deal of chamber music and a one-act opera. It was Douglas Moore who convinced Kander that his talent lay in writing for the popular musical theater.

Leaving Columbia in 1954, Kander served in the United States Army and the United States Merchant Marine Corps. Once out of uniform, he started to make his way in the theater. He gained valuable experience working as the choral director and conductor for the Warwick (Rhode Island) Musical Theater during the summers of 1955 and 1957. Late in 1956 he played the piano for *The Amazing Adele* during its pre-Broadway tryouts, and for Beatrice Lillie's Florida tour. In 1957 he conducted the orchestra for *Conversation Piece* produced at the Barbizon Plaza Theater in New York, and in 1959 and 1960 he made the arrangements of the dance music for the successful Broadway musicals *Gypsy* and *Irma La Douce.*

His Broadway debut as composer came with the musical *The Family Affair,* starring Shelley Berman, on January 27, 1962. With text and lyrics by the Goldman brothers, this was the first musical directed by Harold Prince. *A Family Affair* lasted only sixty performances. Its best songs were "There's a Room in My House," "Beautiful," "Harmony," and the title number. The principal songs from this production were published.

(Like Kander, the Goldman brothers progressed from the failure of *The Family Affair* to immense success, but as screenwriters. Within a few years, James received an Academy Award for his screen-play for *The Lion in Winter,* and William, for *Butch Cassidy and the Sundance Kid.*)

Following the failure of *A Family Affair,* Kander's publisher introduced him to Fred Ebb, a young lyricist in search of a composer. Kander and Ebb became collaborators in 1962, and almost from the very beginning hit it off successfully. Before the year ended they had published "My Coloring Book," a song that became a great hit. Though introduced by Kaye Ballard, it first became popular when Sandy Stewart sang it on Perry Como's television show and then recorded it. Best-selling recordings by Kitty Kallen and particularly by Barbra Streisand followed. In 1963 Kander and Ebb published "I Don't Care Music," introduced and made popular in a Barbra Streisand recording.

During this time Kander and Ebb worked on several musicals, none of which found a producer. Meanwhile, in 1962, Kander wrote incidental music for the successful Broadway play *Never Too Late.*

The debut of Kander and Ebb in the Broadway musical theater took place in 1965 with *Flora, the Red Menace* (a satire on Greenwich Village radicals of the 1930's), with Liza Minnelli in her first appearance on Broadway. The *High Fidelity* reviewer wrote: "This is a fun show that actually is fun, at least as far as the score is concerned. . . . The great merit of *Flora* is that its effervescent score is kept bubbling along by a lively and skillful troupe of singers with the proper talents to make the most of the Ebb and Kander songs." "Unafraid," an exuberant choral number, opened the show whose score included "Dear Love," "A Quiet Thing," "Believe You," and "Knock, Knock."

Flora, the Red Menace was not a success. Kander, however, looks back on it with considerable warmth because he feels the show contained good material, and because he says he learned more about what the musical theater was and should be by watching George Abbott direct the stage production than from any other single influence.

The day after *Flora, the Red Menace* opened (to generally unfavorable reviews), its producer, Harold Prince, asked Kander and Ebb to write the score for a show he was then planning. Prince felt strongly that the two men were worth gambling on, and the gamble paid off handsomely. The projected show was *Cabaret,* a musical comedy adaptation of John van Druten's play *I Am a Camera,* which in turn was based on the Christopher Isherwood stories about a decaying Germany in the years just before the Nazis came to power. Opening on November 20, 1966, with a cast headed by Joel Grey, Lotte Lenya, Jack Gilford, and Jill Haworth, *Cabaret* was a great success. It ran on Broadway for 1,166 performances and captured the Tony and Drama Critics awards as the best musical of the season. The New York Critics poll selected Kander as the leading composer of the season. *Cabaret* was produced in numerous translations throughout Europe, and a national company toured America for several years. To the *Variety* critic this show had "everything. . . . It has bright music, magnificent production numbers, touches of comedy and tragedy, and four different stories vying for audience attention." The title number became a hit song in 1966-1967. Other songs included "If You Could See Her," "It Couldn't Please Me More," "Why Should I Wake Up," "What Would You Do?" and "So What."

The next musical with songs by Kander and Ebb was *The Happy Time,* which opened on Broadway on January 18, 1968. Though far less successful (285 performances) than its distinguished predecessor, it had much to recommend it: excellent performances by Robert Goulet and David Wayne, the brilliant choreography and direction of Gower Champion, and several fine songs. *The Happy Time* was an adaptation of Samuel Taylor's highly successful Broadway play of the same name. It portrayed a French-Canadian family that included a lovable, somewhat lecherous grandfather, his fourteen-year-old grandson with whom the old man maintains a touching relationship, and the boy's uncle who revisits the family in time to straighten out its complications and to fall in love with the local schoolteacher. "A Certain Girl," "Without Me," and "The Life of the Party" were three outstanding musical numbers. The last invariably brought down the house.

Zorba did only slightly better. Opening on November 17, 1968, it lasted on Broadway only twenty performances longer than *The Happy Time*. This musical came out of the best-selling novel, *Zorba the Greek*, which had been made into an exceptional motion picture starring Anthony Quinn. The setting is mainly Crete; the characters are Greeks; the plot concerns an unsuccessful attempt by the young hero to rebuild an abandoned mine he had inherited (a task for which he finds a willing helper in Zorba). Songs similar in style to Cretan music, and Greek dances, were powerful factors in evoking local color, beginning with "Life Is," a frenetic dance with which the production opens. Clive Barnes noted in the New York *Times* that the "ethnic Greek element in the music and the cheerfully philosophical note struck by the lyrics endowed the production with most of its fire and spirit." The score included "Why Can't I Speak?", "Only Love," "The First Time," and "I Am Free." The last expounds Zorba's philosophy of life.

70, Girls, 70, however, lasted only thirty-six performances after opening on April 15, 1971. The book by Fred Ebb and Norman L. Martin was based on a play which had been made into the British motion picture, *Make Mine Mink*. The subject concerned the attempt of some female septuagenarians, all residents of a small West Side hotel in New York, to get adventure in their lives by becoming shoplifters. The songs (lyrics by Fred Ebb), reported Douglas Watts in the *Daily News*, "are mainly brisk and mindless pieces intermixed with sentimental items." They included "Do We?", the amusing "The Elephant Song," and the lively "Broadway My Street."

Kander occupies an apartment on West Seventieth Street in New York City with his wife and two children. Next to writing songs, his main passion is opera. He travels a good deal, primarily to attend for-eign opera performances. He has received a grant from the Ford Foundation to write an opera for the Kansas City Lyric Theater.

ABOUT:

Ewen, D. New Complete Book of the American Musical Theater; Green, S. The World of Musical Comedy (revised edition, 1968).

Gustave Kerker 1857-1923

See *Popular American Composers,* 1962.

Jerome Kern 1885-1945

For biographical sketch and songs see *Popular American Composers,* 1962.

About a dozen of Kern's best-known songs were assembled as background music for a ballet, *You Are Love,* choreography by Jacques d'Amboise. This ballet received its world premiere in Miami, Florida, on February 26, 1971, with d'Amboise and Melissa Hayden dancing the featured roles.

Robert A. King 1862-1932

See *Popular American Composers,* 1962.

Manuel Klein 1876-1919

See *Popular American Composers,* 1962.

Burton Lane 1912-

For biographical sketch and list of earlier songs see *Popular American Composers,* 1962.

In 1964 Lane wrote the music for "Freedom Is the Word" (lyrics by E. Y. Harburg), introduced by Robert Preston and a children's chorus on a closed circuit TV program sponsored by the National Association for the Advancement of Colored People.

Finian's Rainbow, the 1947 hit musical for which Harburg had written the lyrics, was made into a lavish (but commercially unsuccessful) motion picture, released in 1968 and starring Petula Clark and Fred Astaire.

Burton Lane's successful return to the Broadway stage took place on October 17, 1965, with the premiere of *On a Clear Day You Can See Forever,* book and lyrics by Alan Jay Lerner. Lerner had worked with Richard Rodgers on this (under the tentative title of *I Picked a Daisy),* but they disagreed on development of the theme, and that collaboration was dissolved. The story concerns a girl with extrasensory perception and her psychiatrist. In one of her hypnotic trances the girl reveals she is the reincarnation of an eighteenth century wife of a titled Englishman. The psychiatrist falls in love with the eighteenth century girl, but finally settles for the twentieth century girl who discards her own boyfriend for him. The title song became a success after being introduced by Robert Goulet over TV and in a recording. Other standout songs were "Come Back to Me," "Melinda," and "What Did I Have That I Don't Have?" In 1966 *On a Clear Day You Can See Forever* received a Grammy as the best original-cast recording of a musical comedy score. Though Barbara Harris proved herself an enchanting performer in the leading female role, Barbra Streisand was chosen for the part in the motion picture version (costarring Yves Montand), released in June 1970.

In 1967 Lane ended a ten-year term as president of the American Guild of Authors and Composers.

Lane's first wife was Marian Seaman, whom he married on June 28, 1935, and divorced in 1961; they had one child, a daughter. On March 5, 1961, Lane married Lynn Daroff Kaye, the mother of three girls from a previous marriage.

Mitch Leigh 1928-

MITCH LEIGH was born in Brooklyn, New York, on January 30, 1928. He was educated in New York's public schools and received his Bachelor of Arts and Master of Arts degrees from Yale University. There he attended Paul Hindemith's composition class, after having studied music with private teachers for several years.

His professional career in music began in 1954 with the sale of a TV commercial to Revlon. Impressed by the fees he received for this and several more TV commercials, Leigh decided in 1957 to organize Music Makers, Inc., a company specializing in writing musical commercials. As its president and creative director he guided the firm to great financial success. His commercials captured practically every major radio and television award in the field. During this time, Leigh also wrote much ambitious music ranging from jazz to opera. In 1963 he contributed the incidental music for the New York revival of Bernard Shaw's *Too True to Be Good* and, in 1964, for a new Broadway play, *Never Live over a Pretzel Factory.*

His success as a composer for the Broadway theater came with one of the leaders in the history of the American musical theater, *Man of La Mancha,* based on the imaginary exploits of Don Quixote. Its central character alternates between portraying the knight-errant and Cervantes, the author of *Don Quixote.* "I wanted to interweave and merge their identities," explained Dale Wasserman, who wrote the text. "Miguel Cervantes was Don Quixote." The program explained further: "All the characters in the play are imprisoned in a dungeon in Seville at the end of the 16th century. The entire action takes place there and in various other places in the imagination of Miguel de Cervantes." Performed without intermission, the play requires only a single set, with various props superimposed to change the

MITCH LEIGH
Blackstone-Shelburne New York

background in meeting the demands of the plot.

Long before it came to New York, *Man of La Mancha* had originated as a non-musical TV play. Fitted with songs and dances, it was produced at East Haddam, Connecticut, in 1965. Nobody seemed aware of its popular appeal until the musical opened at the ANTA Washington Square Theater, in downtown New York, on November 22, 1965. The critics were ecstatic. Typical of their reaction is this report by Howard Taubman in the New York *Times*: "As Dale Wasserman has written him, Albert Darre directed him, and Richard Kiley plays him, he [Don Quixote and Cervantes], is . . . a mad, gallant, affecting figure who has honestly materialized from the pages of Cervantes. . . . At its best it [*Man of La Mancha*] is audacious in its conception and tasteful in execution."

What followed the opening performance is stage history. *Man of La Mancha* had a New York run of 2,329 performances—the fourth longest in the Broadway musical theater. It received both the New York Drama Critics and the Antoinette Perry (Tony) awards as the season's best musical, the original cast recording was a best seller, and the New York theater sold out for years. By the end of 1970 the show had earned almost five million dollars, returning to its backers a profit of well over 1,000 per cent. In addition, the motion picture and soundtrack recording rights sold for five million dollars, and sheet music sales exceeded two million copies. All the while, companies were performing the show throughout Europe, in Mexico City, Israel, Japan, Australia, and elsewhere—everywhere getting rave reviews. The stars of several of these productions were eventually invited to take over the leading male role at different performances in New York; all of them performed in English. *Man of La Mancha* earned the additional rare distinction (for a Broadway musical) of being included in the opera repertory at the world-famous Komische Oper in East Berlin.

"The Quest," or as it is more commonly known, "The Impossible Dream," has become a standard. "I, Don Quixote" was another of the score's strong assets, a score that made the New York Critics poll select Leigh as the season's leading composer for the Broadway theater.

Leigh's lyricist for *Man of La Mancha* was Joe Darion. They returned to Broadway with *Cry for All of Us*, which Leigh also produced. This musical was based on William Alfred's play *Hogan's Goat*. It opened on April 8, 1970, and had a short run. The plot line was confused and the characters lacked identity. Leigh's score was more pretentious than melodic, more operatic than musical comedy. Clive Barnes referred to it in the New York *Times* as "an inflated bore." From this none-too-distinguished score, the following songs might be singled out: the title number, the "Verandah Waltz," "That Slavery Is Love," and an amusing ditty, "Swing Your Bag."

ABOUT:
Ewen, D. New Complete Book of the American Musical Theater; Green, S. The World of Musical Comedy (revised edition, 1968).

Jay Livingston

Jay Livingston 1915-

For biographical sketch and list of earlier songs see *Popular American Composers,* 1962.

———

Livingston's most important songs since 1962 include: "Dear Heart," written in collaboration with Henry Mancini and Ray Evans, the title number of a motion picture which was nominated for an Academy Award and which was successfully recorded by Andy Williams, by Jack Jones, and by Frank Sinatra; "On My Way," in collaboration with Max Steiner and Ray Evans, the theme song of the motion picture *Youngblood Hawke;* "Never Too Late," written with David Rose and Ray Evans as the title song of the motion picture of the same name, and a song recorded by both Vic Damone and Tony Bennett; "Maybe September," written with Percy Faith and Ray Evans as the theme song for the motion picture *The Oscar,* the song recorded by Tony Bennett; "We've Loved Before," written with Henry Mancini and Ray Evans as the theme music for the motion picture *Arabesque,* and successfully recorded by Henry Mancini and his orchestra; "In the Arms of Love," written with Henry Mancini and Ray Evans for the motion picture *What Did You Do in the War, Daddy?,* the song recorded by Andy Williams and by Henry Mancini and his orchestra; "Green Years," written with John Addison and Ray Evans as the theme for the motion picture *Torn Curtain;* "Wait Until Dark," Livingston again collaborating with Mancini and Evans, used as the title song of a motion picture and recorded by Mel Tormé, by James Darren, by Henry Mancini and his orchestra among others; and "Sugar Boat," written with Ray Evans and recorded by the Mills Brothers.

With Ray Evans, Livingston wrote the theme music for the TV series *To Rome with Love,* produced in 1969-1970.

Jerry Livingston 1909-

JERRY LIVINGSTON was born in Denver, Colorado, on March 25, 1909. He majored in music at the University of Arizona where he became the first freshman ever to write a score for the annual varsity show. At college he also organized and led a jazz band and wrote songs for college productions.

Livingston arrived in New York in 1932 and supported himself by playing the piano with various jazz groups until 1940, when he organized and directed a jazz orchestra of his own. During these eight years, writing songs developed from a hobby into a profession. In 1933 he first achieved some success with his songs, all of which were published. These included "Under a Blanket of Blue" and "It's the Talk of the Town" (lyrics by Marty Symes and Al J. Neiburg); both were performed by Glen Gray and the Casa Loma Orchestra who also recorded it for Decca. Other Livingston songs in the 1930's (lyrics by Symes and Neiburg) were "Invitation to a Dance," which Hal Kemp recorded for Columbia, and "Darkness on the Delta," introduced and recorded by Mildred Bailey.

In 1941 Livingston adapted the main theme from the first movement of Tchaikovsky's *Symphonie pathétique* which, with lyrics by Al Hoffman and Mann Curtis, became "The Story of a Starry Night" and was a best-selling record in 1942 in a performance by Glenn Miller and his orchestra. One of the most successful nonsense songs of the decade was "Mairzy Doats," in 1943, words by Milton Drake and Al Hoffman. Drake arrived at the idea for his lyric, with its apparently unintelligible gibberish after hearing his four-year-old daughter say: "Cowzy tweet and sowzy tweet and liddle sharksy doisters." Drake realized kids liked to slur their words. Then and there he decided to write a song lyric in such a childish manner and enlisted the help of Al Hoffman. Al Trace and his orchestra recorded it, but it was a recording by the

Jerry Livingston

JERRY LIVINGSTON

Merry Macs that first made it popular. Besides becoming a best seller on records, the song did exceedingly well as sheet music with some thirty thousand copies sold every day for several consecutive weeks. The song was revived in the motion picture *A Man Called Peter* in 1955.

Livingston boasted two lesser hit songs in 1943, "What's the Good Word, Mr. Bluebird" (Al Hoffman and Allan Roberts) and "Close to You" (Hoffman), the latter made successful by Frank Sinatra.

Some of Livingston's principal songs in the 1940's were "Fuzzy Wuzzy" (Al Hoffman and Milton Drake); "I'm a Big Girl Now" (Hoffman and Drake); "Chi-Baba, Chi-Baba" (Mack David and Al Hoffman), popularized by Perry Como; "A Dream Is a Wish Your Heart Makes" and "Bibbidi, Bobbidi, Boo," both to lyrics by Mack David and Al Hoffman, both introduced in the full-length Walt Disney cartoon *Cinderella* in 1949, and the latter nominated for an Academy Award and further made popular by Perry Como in his recording; "The Unbirthday Song" (David and Hoffman), used in the Walt Disney full-length cartoon *Alice in Wonderland* in 1951, though the song itself had been written in 1948.

In 1950 Livingston went to Hollywood where, during the next three years, with Mack David as lyricist, he wrote songs for five motion pictures starring Dean Martin and Jerry Lewis. With Mack David he also wrote "Baby, Baby, Baby," which Teresa Brewer sang in the motion picture *Redheads from Seattle* and recorded, and the title song for *Room for One More* starring Cary Grant. Subsequent songs for motion pictures (lyrics to all by Mack David) included "The Hanging Tree," introduced by Marty Robbins in the motion picture of the same name, which was nominated for an Academy Award; "Captain Buffalo" in *Sergeant Rutledge;* and "Cat Ballou," a number that was sung by Nat "King" Cole and Stubby Kaye throughout the film of the same title as a running commentary on the progress of the story.

Livingston has also made prolific contributions to television music. In 1956 he wrote the music for *Jack and the Beanstalk,* a fairy tale special with book and lyrics by Helen Deutsch; it was telecast by NBC. With Mack David as his lyricist, Livingston also wrote songs for Shirley Temple's *Story Book Series.* From 1959 on he wrote title songs with Mack David for numerous series that had varied runs, some of them for several years. These productions included *77 Sunset Strip, Bourbon Street Beat, Hawaiian Eye, Surfside 6, The Roaring Twenties, Bronco, The Alaskans, Friendly Ghost,* and *Lawman.*

While working for the movies and television, Livingston kept producing hit songs not written for any specific production but which nevertheless enjoyed wide circulation. The most important were "Wake Up the Town and Tell the People" (Sammy Gallop) which Les Baxter and his orchestra recorded; "The Twelfth of Never" (Paul Francis Webster), melody taken from the Kentucky folksong, "The Riddle Song," the Livingston-Webster version made famous in a recording by Johnny Mathis, and the song itself the recipient of a special

61

Award of Merit from ASCAP; "Bluebell" and "Periwinkle Blue," both with lyrics by Paul Francis Webster, the former recorded by Mitch Miller and his orchestra, and the latter by Doris Day; and "Young Emotions" (Mack David) which Ricky Nelson made into a best-selling recording in 1962.

ABOUT:
ASCAP Biographical Dictionary (1966).

Frank Loesser 1910-1969

For biographical sketch and list of earlier songs see *Popular American Composers,* 1962.

———

How to Succeed in Business Without Really Trying (1961) turned out to be Loesser's most successful musical comedy. It had a run of 1,147 performances (the sixth longest-running production on Broadway up to then), became the fourth Broadway musical to capture the Pulitzer Prize (the first time this honor came to Loesser), and the second musical to get the Theater Club Award as the best play of the season by an American. It won a Tony and the New York Drama Critics Circle award as the season's best musical. The motion picture adaptation (starring Robert Morse and Rudy Vallee of the original stage cast) was released in 1967 and proved to be one of the year's major box office draws.

In 1965 Loesser wrote the words and music for *Pleasures and Palaces,* which closed out of town.

A victim of cancer, Frank Loesser died at Mount Sinai Hospital in New York on July 28, 1969. He had been working on a new musical when he was hospitalized four weeks before his death. In accordance with his own request, Loesser's body was cremated and the ashes scattered over the sea. He was survived by his second wife, the former Jo Sullivan who had starred in *Most Happy Fella,* and whom he had married in 1957. They

had two daughters. Loesser's first marriage was to Lynn Garland in 1936, with whom he had two sons.

In December 1970, almost a year and a half after his death, Loesser's musical play *Greenwillow* (1960) was revived Off Broadway by the Equity Library Theater to unfavorable reviews.

Frederick Loewe 1904-

For biographical sketch and list of earlier songs see *Popular American Composers,* 1962.

———

The screen adaptation of *My Fair Lady,* with Audrey Hepburn in the female lead and Rex Harrison playing the role he created in the original Broadway production, was one of the most successful movies of the years following its release by Warner Brothers in 1964. *Camelot* (1960) was filmed in 1967 in a splendid and also highly successful Warner Brothers production. Eighteen years after it had first been produced on Broadway with only minor success, *Paint Your Wagon* (1951) was made by Paramount into a motion picture with a cast including Lee Marvin, Harve Presnell, and Jean Seberg and a screen adaptation by Alan Jay Lerner. In addition to the original stage score, the film included several new numbers with words by Alan Jay Lerner and music by André Previn. Though lavishly produced, the motion picture was not a success.

John D. Loudermilk 1934-

IN PRODUCING a copious repertory of country and western music from "Music City, U.S.A." (Nashville, Tennessee), Loudermilk has often drawn his subjects from personal experiences. He has a rich source to tap since at different times in his life he worked as a carpenter's assistant, steam-shovel oiler, messenger boy for a telegraph company, clerk in a department store, tobacco farmer, factory laborer,

JOHN D. LOUDERMILK

janitor, shoeshine boy, lifeguard, cotton-gin employee, door-to-door salesman of Bibles, sign painter, window dresser, employee in a hosiery mill, commercial artist, TV cameraman and entertainer, and photographer. An advertisement for one of his concerts was, then, thoroughly justified in maintaining that he is a man "who writes and sings of everything he sees, hears, feels, tastes and smells"; that he is a man "who feels the rhythm of life and wants to share it"; that his songs "depict every environment, every song-of-life he sees."

John D. Loudermilk (the "D" does not represent any name) was born in Durham, North Carolina, on March 31, 1934. He came from an impoverished family, the only boy among three children. His father was a carpenter who could neither read nor write. "I used to go to the grocery store with him on Saturday afternoon," recalls Loudermilk, "and sign his paycheck for him." About his mother he has written: "Mother was a housewife and a sweet and wonderful mother but, bless her heart, she liked to move a lot. She seemed happiest when the big moving van was backing up to the porch and the pasteboard boxes started to move. From the time I can first remember to the time

I left home we moved nineteen times and never got out of the same school district." He adds: "Man, I knew total poverty." Today he does not regard this as any kind of handicap, explaining: "When all you've got to look forward to as a kid is going downtown and buying a $400 suede coat, you're worse off spiritually than that kid who knows he's got to strive like hell to eat."

Loudermilk did such striving from his early boyhood on, taking any job he could find to help support his family, even while he was in elementary school. His first musical experience was singing hymns in church, attending Saturday night barn dances, and listening to the Grand Ole Opry radio programs. He made his first public appearance in early childhood when he and his mother sang and played "Life's a Railway to Heaven" in church. His professional debut on the *Judy Martin Show* over the local radio station WTIK came when he was eleven. A year later, Loudermilk made his TV debut on WTV in Durham, on a show with Tex Ritter as master of ceremonies. When Loudermilk was thirteen he had a radio show of his own where he was identified as "Johnny Dee." He also played at square dances and toured with a local jazz group. His basic music training came from playing in the Salvation Army band. Though the only music education he had thus far were some lessons on the guitar, he played the saxophone, guitar, trumpet, and bass drum in this band. Many of the hymns and gospels the Salvation Army band performed he has never forgotten; one of them ("When the Roll Is Called") influenced the melody of one of his later successful songs, "Waterloo."

Loudermilk attended public schools in Durham, Campbell College in Buies Creek, North Carolina, and for a time the University of North Carolina, at the same time that he drifted from one job to another. His favorite avocation now was writing music, and when he was not doing that he was reading voraciously, especially the poetry of Edgar A. Guest and James Metcalfe whose influence can be detected in his later lyric writing.

After graduating from high school, he worked at the Durham TV station painting sets and supplemented his small salary by doing some outside commercial art work. He also played the bass fiddle in the studio combo an hour a day, and once in a while was called upon to do a solo number on the guitar. "It was during this time that I discovered the works of Kahlil Gibran, the Eastern poet and philosopher, who inspired me to try my hand at writing. One night after work I wrote a poem about a rose and a Baby Ruth candy bar. It sounded pretty good, so I put a tune to it with my guitar." He sang it one day over WTVD and was heard by George Hamilton IV, a young college student from the University of North Carolina, who became excited by the song. Hamilton managed to record it for ABC-Paramount in 1956. This recording made the then unknown Hamilton a recording star; and it brought Loudermilk his first success as a composer-lyricist. Since its original recording, "A Rose and a Baby Ruth" has sold over four million disks.

Loudermilk next wrote "Sittin' in the Balcony," which both Eddie Cochran and Loudermilk recorded. Both releases were successes (Cochran's was his first solid hit). Loudermilk dropped out of college and returned to his native city. There he fell in love with Gwen Cooke, a music major at Duke University, whom he induced to leave college and marry him. They were married in the same chapel in Durham which Loudermilk's father had helped to build. The marriage later ended in divorce after the Loudermilks had raised three sons.

Convinced of his songwriting talent, Loudermilk established his home in Nashville, Tennessee. There he became affiliated with the Cedarwood Publishing Company which issued his first songs. He also became friendly with the celebrated guitarist and one of the musical powers in Nashville, Chet Atkins, who would be an all-important influence in advancing Loudermilk's career.

Loudermilk's songs were still being published by Cedarwood and still being recorded. Among his first successes in Nashville was "Tobacco Road" (recalling Loudermilk's boyhood experiences), which in 1964 became one of the best record sellers in England, "Amigo's Guitar," and "Grin and Bear It."

In 1961 Loudermilk left Cedarwood for the influential Nashville house Acuff-Rose, Inc., with whom he has remained. Since 1961 he has written and published over five hundred songs (words and music). Sixteen received awards from BMI, and fourteen sold a million or more records each. In 1968 Loudermilk received a Grammy for his album *Suburban Attitudes in Country Verse* which (as the title indicates) is made up of poems rather than songs.

Loudermilk's most popular songs include the following: "Sad Movies," "Norman," "Hollywood," "Ebony Eyes," "Dreamboat," "Stayin' In," "Thou Shalt Not Steal," "Torture," "James," "I Can't Hang Up the Phone," "Bad News," "Talk Back, Trembling Lips," "Abilene," "Break My Mind," "Then You Can Tell Me Goodbye," "I Wanna Live," "Fort Worth, Dallas or Houston," "That Ain't All," "Waterloo," "Everything's All Right," "Paper Tiger," "The Little Grave," "To Hell with Love," and "Joey Stays with Me." Some of these were made highly successful by such recording artists as Connie Francis, Bobby Vee, George Hamilton IV, Sue Thompson, Chet Atkins, and the Everly Brothers.

The variety of subjects dealt with in his songs is pointed up by his album *John D. Loudermilk Sings a Bizarre Collection of the Most Unusual Songs*, released in 1967. A reviewer for *Hi-Fi Stereo* said: "Here's a record from Nashville that lives up to its title. The genial, folksy Mr. Loudermilk tackles the most curious ballads—ditties on such off-beat subjects as a Southern lady who won't sell her house to make way for the TVA, a child who is ordered not to play in the snow because a news item reports it's radioactive, and a fellow suffering agonies of guilt over a pheasant he shot on Christmas Eve. There's a talking blues, about an affluent rock 'n' roll singer who has his revenge on an automobile salesman who refuses to wait on him, a tirade against the artificiality of a world made up of paper plates and plastic spoons, and a catchy little number about a happy bum walkin' and cussin' down an immaculate new highway. There are also a few sticky songs of a sentimental nature, but these are balanced by unexpected pieces like 'To Hell with Love.' "

In some of his love songs ("Talk Back, Trembling Lips," "Language of Love," "Little World Girl") Loudermilk writes about the problems of the young. "Going to Hell" is a protest against the world's complacency towards existing evils. In "I'm Looking for a World" he berates phoniness through the complaints of a girl who is bored with paper dolls, artificial flowers, and plastics. *Windy and Warm* is an instrumental which Chet Atkins made famous.

When Jesse Burt interviewed Loudermilk in 1968 he found him "tall, clear-eyed, well-barbered, wearing a conventional white shirt, conventional necktie, and conventional footwear, but no hat. His brownish hair obviously was his own, and it bore the traces of the Florida and Caribbean sun."

Loudermilk's interests are many and varied: from boating and astrology to tracing the course of hurricanes; from playing pool to watching the constellations through telescopes; from dabbling with commercial art to motorcycling; from reading poetry to studying occult writings. About his fascination for hurricanes he has written: "I've been to every hurricane on the Atlantic Coast since Hurricane Hazel. I enjoy trying to anticipate the storm's erratic movement, and being at the spot where it comes ashore

is a gas. During emergency situations like these, people of all classes huddle together and the long hours of conversation and fellowship are enlightening."

Cartoons, photos, sketches, ideas for songs, fan mail, and newspaper clippings clutter the walls of Loudermilk's studio at his home in the Brentwood colony of Nashville. Jesse Burt further informs us: "John's inner lair is papered with authentic charts used by sea captains. The genuine leather chairs are deep and comfortable. As a conversation piece, John has on his desk a box filled with fossilized shark's teeth from the Indian Ocean. To his right hangs a 'No Smoking' sign, but John D. isn't a militant nonsmoker; visitors may light up. The sign is there to remind John D. that he kicked fags . . . years ago, partly to set a positive example to his three sons."

Though Acuff-Rose has remained the publisher of Loudermilk's songs, he founded a publishing house of his own in Nashville in 1968—Windward Side. Until 1969 Loudermilk confined his singing to recordings on the RCA Victor label. Since then he has also given concerts —singing, playing on instruments, and speaking to his audiences about things that happen to be on his mind at the moment.

ABOUT:

Stambler, I. and Landon, G. Encyclopedia of Folk, Country, and Western Music.
Nashville Magazine, April 1968.

Gustav Luders 1865-1913

See *Popular American Composers*, 1962.

Jimmy McHugh 1895-1969

For biographical sketch and earlier songs see *Popular American Composers*, 1962.

In 1960 McHugh wrote the music for "Where the Hot Wind Blows" (words by Buddy Kaye), introduced on the soundtrack of a French-Italian motion picture of the same name. A year later, McHugh honored Mrs. John F. Kennedy in the song "The First Lady Waltz" (lyrics by Ned Washington). From 1962 until his death McHugh was vice-president of ASCAP, and at the time of his death he served as assistant secretary.

Jimmy McHugh died at his home in Beverly Hills, California, on May 23, 1969. "When they talk about great composers," said Stanley Adams, president of ASCAP, during the funeral services in Beverly Hills on May 27, "the talk is meaningless unless the name of Jimmy McHugh is mentioned among the elite, the royalty of songdom, the Titans of Tin Pan Alley."

In June 1970 the School of Performing Arts at the University of Southern California initiated an annual Jimmy McHugh cash award for composition to the student composer submitting the best original musical work that year in any medium of his choice.

Rod McKuen 1933-

AMONG popular-song composers few can rival Rod McKuen's versatility. He is the most commercially successful poet America has produced, the only one who has sold over three and a half million copies of his poems and lyrics in hard cover. In addition to his career as a poet, he has been an illustrator, motion picture actor, disk jockey, performer (of both his own songs and of folk music) whose concerts sell out auditoriums, composer of serious music (including a piano concerto and several works for orchestra), and prolific creator of a library of popular songs for which he wrote both the lyrics and the music. "The real me," he told an interviewer, "isn't the poetry or the lyrics or the music. It's all part of a mosaic."

McKuen was born in Oakland, California, on April 29, 1933. He never knew his father, who had deserted his family soon after Rod was born. His mother kept

ROD McKUEN

Helen Milljakovich

moving from one western state to another, working as a waitress, a dance-hall hostess, a telephone operator, and a hasher. Wherever she went she took along her two sons. Rod had little formal academic education, dropping out of school early in life and not returning to the classroom until his adult years, and then only briefly. In all he had only four and a half years of schooling.

His mother married a construction worker for whom Rod had little affection or sympathy. Rod ran away from home when he was eleven, traveling about picking up odd jobs, including those of lumberjack, cookie cutter, logger, cattle herder, rod man on a surveyor unit, and bulldogger with a rodeo. By the time he was seventeen he was back in Oakland working as singer and disk jockey at radio station KROW. There he began reading his poems and singing his songs, winning the Blue Ribbon Award of the San Francisco *Examiner* as the most promising newcomer to radio. Encouraged by his listeners, McKuen became a prolific writer, working on his poems (some of which he set to music) eighteen hours a day. What he knew about music he learned by studying textbooks on theory and composition. While working for radio he also wrote a syndicated column, *Scribblings on My Shirtcuff.*

In 1953 he was drafted into the United States Army. Dispatched to Japan, he wrote psychological warfare scripts. When off duty he appeared as a singer at a Ginza Strip supper club in Tokyo. He also managed to act in six motion pictures filmed in Japan. In Korea, his next station, he served as an American aid administrator for the Korean Civil Assistance Command.

He was discharged from the Army in 1955. In San Francisco, through the influence of Phyllis Diller (whom he first met at KROW where she had worked as copywriter) he got a job at the nightspot *Purple Onion* singing ballads at intermission time. His limited repertory compelled him to write ballads of his own which found favor with his audiences. He was discovered there by the gossip columnist Cobina Wright, Sr., who arranged for him to appear in a Hollywood nightclub, and after that found a place for him in the motion picture and television industries. Between 1956 and 1958 he worked on the Universal-International lot, appearing in four films and doing the scores for some of them. There he attracted the interest of Henry Mancini, Sonny Burke, and others whose encouragement led him to try to promote himself as a songwriter. One of his first hits was "Sing Boy, Sing," which he wrote with Tommy Sands who recorded it and sang it in the motion picture of the same name.

In 1959 McKuen came to New York to promote one of his records. He intended to stay only a week but remained four years. At first he had to sell blood to raise rent money, and to "crash" sales conventions at the Waldorf-Astoria Hotel in order to eat. Eventually he was able to support himself adequately by writing music and serving as conductor for Albert McCleary's CBS Workshop, and by writing special material for performing artists. A tongue-in-cheek takeoff on Chubby Checker, "Oliver Twist," now became his

first hit, selling about a million copies. He was also beginning to make a reputation as a singer, first at Trude Heller's discothèque, and after that in the lounge of the Copacabana nightclub. At the latter spot he was required to perform four shows a night, seven nights a week. This was followed by an eight-week tour of eighty cities, where he appeared mainly in bowling alleys with a five-piece combo. At this time his was a strong baritone voice. But the strain on his vocal chords from his numerous appearances proved so great that his doctors warned that if he continued maintaining so strenuous a schedule he was in danger of losing not only his singing but even his speaking voice.

To give his voice the rest it required, he returned to Hollywood and devoted himself to writing poems and songs. His first volume of poems was *Stanyan Street and Other Sorrows,* which McKuen published at his own expense because it was turned down by so many publishers. (This was not his first book of poetry. *And Autumn Came* was published in 1953 by a vanity press and passed unnoticed.) It achieved the remarkable sale of 65,000 copies, the largest of any book of poems in two decades according to the New York *Times.* Later, when the New York publishing company Random House acquired the reprint rights, the sales of this volume became even greater. Random House has since published other volumes of McKuen's poems, including *In Someone's Shadow, Listen to the Warm, Lonesome Cities, The World of Rod McKuen, The World of Rod McKuen II, Caught in the Quiet,* and *Fields of Wonder.* In 1968 McKuen became the only author to have three albums of his poems on the best-selling record lists, with *Lonesome Cities* selling over a million albums and receiving a Grammy in the category of "the spoken word."

Meanwhile, in 1963, McKuen visited Paris where he became interested in and developed his later *chansonnier* style—a soft, relaxed, murmurous way of singing which soon brought him success as a performer both in Europe and America.

In Hollywood, McKuen also worked intensively on songwriting. Extraordinarily prolific, he produced seventy-nine songs in one month in 1965. Many of his songs became best sellers in recordings by Eddy Arnold, the Limelighters, the Kingston Trio, Glenn Yarbrough, Jimmie Rodgers, and others. In 1969 Frank Sinatra recorded an album of McKuen's songs entitled *A Man Alone*. Other artists who recorded albums of his songs have been Petula Clark (*Because We Love*), Glenn Yarbrough (*Each of Us Alone, The Rod McKuen Song Book,* and *The Lonely Things*), Don Ho, in collaboration with McKuen (*The Two of Us*), and Anita Kerr, in collaboration with McKuen (*The Earth*). But Rod McKuen has perhaps been his own best song salesman, in a long series of albums that have enjoyed great success. He signed an exclusive contract with RCA Victor in 1965, his first album for that company, *Rod McKuen Sings His Own*, immediately making the best-seller lists. Since then his numerous albums have amassed extraordinary sales figures, some of them passing the million mark.

McKuen has written about a thousand songs, such as "The World I Used to Know," "If You Go Away," "Town and Country," "So Long, Stay Well," "One by One," "Love's Been Good to Me," "A Crack in the Liberty Bell," "Rusting in the Rain," "Everything But the Truth," "The Living End," "The Flower Generation," "It Gets Lonesome When Love Goes," "The Summertime of Days," "In a Lonely Place," "Before the Monkeys Came," "Zangra," "The Single Man," "A Man Alone," "I'll Catch the Sun," "The Girls of Summer," "Some Trust in Chariots," and "So Long, San Francisco."

His success as a performer of his songs has matched his success as a creator. He has been heard in leading nightclubs, music halls, theaters, casinos, and concert auditoriums in America and Europe.

He was invited to perform for President Rhee of Korea, Queen Elizabeth of England (twice), President John F. Kennedy at State dinners at the White House (twice). On April 28 and 29, 1970, his concerts at the Lincoln Center for the Performing Arts in New York, held in honor of his thirty-seventh birthday, were promptly sold out. On August 18, 1970, his audience overtaxed the capacity of the auditorium at the Saratoga Performing Arts Center. On May 24, 1970, he had been his own severest competition in London by appearing in person at the Palladium at the same time that he participated on tape in a BBC-TV production. In the United States he was the star of two TV specials, *The World of Rod McKuen* and, in January 1971, *Say Goodbye* which he narrated. In his singing appearances he favors an unusual costume comprising sneakers, a sweatshirt (or crewneck sweater), and chinos (or black trousers).

He gives about eighty concerts a year throughout the United States, favoring auditoriums with seating capacities not exceeding three thousand or so. Nevertheless, a ten-concert outdoor tour during the summer of 1970 attracted over a quarter of a million ticket buyers. For these concerts he has not only adopted the strange costume described above but also a most carefree, informal manner. He begins with a song. Then he sits on a stool and for the next two hours he sings some forty numbers, recites some of his poems, speaks the lines of his lyrics to musical accompaniment or recites his own poems to a musical background, tells jokes, and makes verbal comments on a variety of subjects. After his encores, he holds an improvised session for less than an hour during which he answers questions on personal, political, or social matters.

He sings in a hoarse, relaxed voice as if he were exchanging personal confidences with his listeners. One critic said he sounded like "he gargled with Dutch Cleanser." Influenced by the French traditions of presenting *chansons*, McKuen has brought to his singing style simplicity, intensity, and intimacy. His fascination for French popular songs has led him to adapt for American audiences some numbers by Jacques Brel, including the highly successful "If You Go Away." (Jacques Brel has returned the favor by adapting McKuen's "The Lovers" into a French hit song, *"Les Amants de Coeur."*) French songwriting mannerisms are frequently introduced in his own creative efforts. "By now," McKuen has confessed, "our [Jacques Brel's and my] styles in writing . . . are so entwined, it's hard to tell who derived the inspiration from whom."

McKuen's own songs often touch upon his experiences in love and travel, his loneliness and volatile moods, his reactions to social currents, his opinions of political figures and people in the news. After McKuen's first concert in 1970, John S. Wilson wrote: "He rasped out his songs, sentimental laments of loneliness and love, some with an implication of hope, some carrying a sense of defeat. . . . There was, in Mr. McKuen's songs and in his poems, something of the simple warmth of O. Henry without the trick endings, and a kind of sentimentality that often made him sound like a hip Edgar Guest. But he projected such unadorned sincerity that even the manifest corn in his material became effectively communicative."

"I have enormous respect," wrote a record critic in *Hi-Fi Stereo Review.* "Reasons: he has the guts to ignore the trends and fads which insist a performer must sing brainless trash to make music. . . . He has taste; his songs tell stories about life the way he knows it, which is all anyone can ask of an artist. He is a sort of Hart Crane of pop music. . . . The man knows what his life is about."

McKuen has written songs for several motion pictures. "Jean," from *The Prime of Miss Jean Brodie,* was nominated for an Academy Award in 1969 and received the Foreign Press Association Golden Globe Award as the best song of the year in 1970. In 1969 McKuen wrote the words

and music of "Joanna" for *I'll Catch the Sun,* and the lyrics for the title number of *Me, Natalie* (music by Henry Mancini). In collaboration with several others, he wrote words and music for *A Boy Named Charlie Brown,* released in 1970, whose title song was nominated for an Academy Award. In 1970 he also made his debut as a producer-director in motion pictures with *Chuck,* starring Rock Hudson. In 1971 he wrote and performed the songs for the film *Scandalous John.*

Six feet tall, McKuen gives the impression of being shorter because of an habitual slouch. His blue eyes are reflective, contributing the only softness to an otherwise strong and rugged face. One senses at once that this is a lonely man. McKuen likes to keep moving all the time from place to place, a man without roots. Nevertheless he owned a comfortable home, a compact stucco house overlooking San Fernando Valley in Los Angeles, comprising a living room, dining area, two bedrooms, kitchen, and a huge workroom where he kept a library of over 12,000 records and the barber chair which his press agent gave him. "I hole up at the house days at a time," he told an interviewer. "It's got to be comfortable. I believe in comfort." He has since acquired a thirty-room mansion in Regency style in Beverly Hills. His offices on Sunset Strip are far more modest. Here a dozen employees attend to his varied business affairs, including the direction of two music publishing companies, a record company, and a book publishing venture.

He is a lover of animals and keeps a large sheep dog as constant companion, while maintaining a ménage of other dogs as well as cats. The collection of records (in addition to those at home he has eight thousand in storage) and paintings are major interests. The walls of his home reflect the variety of his taste in art—abstract paintings, pop art, advertising posters, and masterworks. His main outdoor activity is walking, and though he is basically a "loner" he does manage to do some dating. Since he requires little sleep (no more than five hours), he puts in a sixteen-hour day in work since he prefers working to loafing.

ABOUT:

Stambler, I. and Landon, G. Encyclopedia of Folk, Country, and Western Music.

New York Times Magazine, April 4, 1971; Newsweek, November 4, 1968; Redbook, November 1968.

Henry Mancini 1924-

HENRY MANCINI was born on April 16, 1924, in Cleveland, Ohio, where his father, a steelworker, was an amateur flutist. During Henry's childhood, the Mancini family moved to Aliquippa, Pennsylvania. There, in his eighth year, Henry began to study the flute and piccolo. He was an adept student. Before long he was sufficiently competent at both instruments to be able to join the Sons of Italy Band of which his father was a member. Mancini confesses today that he was not then overly interested in music; that, indeed, he greatly resented the time he had to spend practising and taking lessons instead of playing football. But his father was determined to keep him at music study and when Henry reached thirteen, his father insisted that he take piano lessons as well.

Henry's love for music suddenly emerged when he heard recordings of the big-name jazz bands of the 1940's. He became infatuated with jazz, and Artie Shaw became his idol. One of Henry's greatest pleasures was to write out Artie Shaw's jazz arrangements after listening to his recordings. He pursued this hobby not only at home but, from memory, even in the classroom. Then he found a new idol: Glenn Miller and his orchestra. Infected with the jazz virus, he joined local jazz combos as flutist. In 1937 he won first prize as flutist of the Pennsylvania All-State Band.

Mancini took lessons in composition and theory from Max Adkins, a conductor of and arranger for a theater orchestra. While still attending high school he con-

HENRY MANCINI

tinued his music study at the School of Music of the Carnegie Institute of Technology. He was graduated from high school in 1942, and his class yearbook described him as "a true music lover, collects records, plays in the band and has even composed several beautiful selections. He hopes someday to have his own orchestra."

One day he sent some of his jazz arrangements to Benny Goodman who not only bought one of them but advised Mancini to come to New York and work for him. This arrangement did not work out very well, since Mancini was not yet ready to undertake so demanding an assignment. Realizing that he needed to learn more about music before embarking upon a professional career, Mancini enrolled in the Juilliard School of Music. Before he could get the kind of musical training he sought, he was drafted into the Army and sent overseas for war duty in the infantry and air corps.

In 1945, after his discharge from the Army, Mancini found a job as pianist and arranger with the Glenn Miller Orchestra which, since Miller's death during the war, was led by Tex Beneke. Mancini remained with the orchestra for three years. During this time, in 1947, he married a young singer, Virginia O'Connor.

After leaving the Glenn Miller Orchestra, Mancini took on whatever assignment came along as arranger for singer and jazz groups. This continued for four difficult years, his income barely enough to support his family, which by 1950 included a son.

In 1952 he was signed by Universal-International to write some music for one of their motion pictures. The contract required his services for two weeks, but he stayed on the lot six years. During this period he wrote music for more than one hundred motion pictures. All this was basically hack work, but it gave Mancini a valuable apprenticeship in learning the motion picture business and the techniques and methods of writing music for the films.

Two important screen productions gave him his first opportunity to demonstrate the scope of his musical ability, particularly in the area of jazz. One was *The Glenn Miller Story* in 1954, which brought him his first Academy Award nomination and which was, for Mancini, a labor of love. His second important motion picture was *The Benny Goodman Story* in 1956. There is a third picture of whose music Mancini is proud, *The Touch of Evil,* directed by Orson Welles in 1957; a decade later this was regarded as an "art film" deserving revival in colleges throughout the country.

A fellow employee of his at Universal-International was Blake Edwards. When Edwards was promoted to director, he engaged Mancini to write the music for his productions. This affiliation led to a lasting friendship as well as a profound mutual admiration. When, in 1958, Blake was hired to prepare *Peter Gunn,* a series for television, he asked Mancini to do the background music. Utilizing a small ensemble since funds were limited, Mancini wrote background music strongly influenced by the jazz idiom, music with a pronounced jazz beat and melodies often in a blues style. His music attracted considerable attention. Blake Edwards was one of the first to concede that much of the enormous appeal of Peter Gunn was due to the effectiveness of the background music. The recurring theme identifying this series sold over one million records in a release made by Ray Anthony. Mancini used some of the basic music from the series and recorded it with his own orchestra. This album also became a best seller (over one million albums were sold), besides capturing two Grammys as the best record album of the year, and as the year's best arrangement. Mancini was also awarded an Emmy for his *Peter Gunn* music.

Mancini's next assignment for Blake Edwards was to prepare music for a second television series, *Mr. Lucky.* This production failed to make the grade with television ratings and was dropped. Mancini's music, however, was not ignored. It brought him two more Grammys, and became a best seller in a recording by Mancini and his orchestra.

In 1960 Mancini returned to Hollywood to work for the screen as a freelance composer. He was no longer looked upon as a hack hired hand, nor was he any longer the apprentice. This was proved during the three ensuing years with his outstanding background music for *High Time, Bachelor in Paradise, Breakfast at Tiffany's,* and *Days of Wine and Roses. Breakfast at Tiffany's* (starring Audrey Hepburn in an adaptation of Truman Capote's story) brought Mancini his first Oscar for the song "Moon River" (words by Johnny Mercer) which sold more than two million disks in Andy Williams' recording. It subsequently became Andy Williams' musical signature on his own television series, and received several Grammys, including one as the best song of the year.

"Moon River" was Mancini's first hit song. In time it received over five hundred different recordings, sold over a million copies of sheet music, and earned for Mancini and Mercer more than $250,000 each in royalties.

For "Days of Wine and Roses,"—title number of a motion picture—Mancini won his second Oscar in a row. Once again Mercer was his lyricist; once again Andy Williams recorded it, this time in an album that carried the name of the song and sold over a million copies; once again it earned a Grammy as the song of the year together with several more Grammys. Meanwhile, in 1962, Mancini conceived the background music for the motion picture *Hatari,* from which came the songs "Just for Tonight" and "Soldier in the Rain" (Mercer).

Following "Days of Wine and Roses," between 1963 and 1965 Mancini was three times nominated for an Academy Award for his songs: for "Charade" (lyrics by Mercer), from the motion picture of the same name; for "Dear Heart" (lyrics by Jay Livingston and Ray Evans), also a title number; and for "Sweetheart Tree" (words by Mercer), from *The Great Race.* In 1964 he was nominated for an Oscar for his background music to *The Pink Panther;* for this production Mancini (in collaboration with Mercer and Franco Misliacci) wrote the song "It Had Better Be Tonight."

Among the subsequent motion pictures for which Mancini wrote background music, and sometimes songs, were *A Shot in the Dark; Experiment in Terror; Wait until Dark; Moment to Moment; Darling Lili,* whose best songs were "Whistling Away the Dark" (which received the Golden Globe Award of the Foreign Press Association in 1970 as the year's best motion picture song and was nominated for an Academy Award), "The Girl in No Man's Land," and "Smile Away Each Rainy Day" (Mercer); *Me, Natalie,* for whose songs Rod McKuen wrote the lyrics; *Gaily, Gaily; Sunflower,* an Italian-made motion picture which was nominated for an Academy Award in 1971 for its scoring; *The Hawaiians;* and *Sometimes a Great Notion.*

In 1969 Mancini received a Grammy for his instrumental arrangement of the love theme from *Romeo and Juliet;* in 1969-1970 his recording with his orchestra of *Warmer Shade of Love* sold over a million albums; and in 1970 his recording for RCA Victor of the theme from *Love Story* was selected by *Cash Box* and *Record World* magazine as "the pick of the week." In 1971 Mancini received a Grammy for his recording of the theme from the motion picture *Z,* in the category of best instrumental arrangement. Mancini, however, did not himself compose any of the above-mentioned music.

Mancini's gift for a fresh and personal lyricism in his hit songs is matched only by his ability to be thoroughly original in his background music in conception, methods, and use of unorthodox instruments. Even scores that failed to produce song hits are, as the editor of this book says in *Great Men of American Popular Song,* "overstocked with treasurable melodic thoughts which will someday acquire lyrics, be revived, and emerge as prime favorites." The discussion of Mancini's special talent for screen background music continues: "The relevance of his music to the incident, episode, or background for which it was intended must . . . be noted. . . . Mancini's writing is vividly programmatic as he seeks out the precise music that does full justice to, or enhances, the scene being projected on the screen. In his search for the musical *mot juste,* in his insistence on musical realism, Mancini is not afraid to employ the most unusual effects and instruments, and he often does so with remarkable results. He used a calliope for a most descriptive amusing little tune, to a boogie-woogie rhythm, as background music for a scene in *Hatari* in which a girl is being followed by a baby elephant, while for the recurring theme in the same movie he made use of an untuned piano. He brought a homespun fascination to 'Moon River' when it was played by an amplified harmonica. In *Experiment in Terror* he employed a leitmotif for the villain, strummed on (of all things!) an autoharp, contributing thereby not a little to the atmosphere of terror being projected. In *Wait Until Dark* he introduced into the orchestra an ancient Chinese instrument of the flute family, a Sho, whose haunting, exotic sounds were just what these episodes called for."

For his background music for *The Hawaiians* (which he also conducted) he had to use three separate musical ideas. He describes them as follows: "First there is the Oriental, accompanying the opening sequences showing the arrival of the Chinese laborers in the islands; then the Hawaiian-flavored passages for scenes involving the islands' queen, and, finally, a dramatic background for the finale which depicts the burning of the Chinese section of Honolulu. But none of this music ever becomes dominant in the picture. It was the director's opinion that this was not the type of story which called for heavy musical accent. And I agreed. We sought a subtle approach so that the music would augment the drama, but would never call attention to itself."

Before beginning to work on background music or songs, he views the movie four or five times, taking profuse notes and keeping the action fixed in his mind. Then, when he starts writing his music, he does not look at the picture again until his work is done. He works primarily at the piano.

In discussing the art and science of writing background music, Mancini revealed: "Sometimes there'll be just a basic theme like in *The Pink Panther*. It'll run all the way through in different settings. In other cases you'll have various individual songs. Some of these we call source music because they're actually made by a band or a singer, in other words, a source that you can see in the picture. In *Breakfast at Tiffany's* there are four or five of these in the party scene alone. . . . When I approach a film I always think cinematically. I want to do my job for the picture honestly. I always approach a score as to what is best for the picture—not what's best for a record album, or the shortest cut to a hit song. That's the reason why so many of my scores—however effective they might be as part of a film—are unsuitable

for recordings, since they consist of fragments."

In 1971 Mancini once again worked for television by writing the background music for a special, *Curiosity Shop*, telecast over the ABC network.

The Mancinis have three children: twin daughters born in 1952, besides their son. They live in the Holmby Hills section of Los Angeles. Mancini dresses as he lives, in simple dignity. He is no party man, nor an habitué of Beverly Hills cocktail parties. His passion is sailing on his thirty-foot cruiser. Other interests include skiing, swimming, collecting art, talking shop with musicians, and just loafing around at home with his family.

He has given numerous concerts with his orchestra in nightclubs and auditoriums, and has written a guide to professional orchestration, *Sounds and Scores*. His interest in his profession has led him to endow a chair at the University of California at Los Angeles in screen music composition to help young musicians learn the techniques of what he regards as "a very delicate craft." Between 1970 and 1971 he established two more scholarships, one of which is an annual award to an outstanding student of composition at the Juilliard School of Music.

ABOUT:
Ewen, D. Great Men of American Popular Song.

Hugh Martin 1914-

For biographical sketch and list of earlier songs see *Popular American Composers,* 1962.

With the collaboration of Timothy Gray, Martin wrote the book, lyrics, and music for the successful Broadway musical *High Spirits*, based on Noel Coward's stage play *Blithe Spirit*. Starring Beatrice Lillie as the eccentric medium in a satire on spiritualism, *High Spirits* opened on Broadway on April 7, 1964. Among the principal songs were "Home Sweet Heaven," "Where Is the Man I Married?", and "If I Gave You."

Tattered Tom—book by Timothy Gray and lyrics and music by Ralph Blane and Hugh Martin—was a failure after opening in New York on November 29, 1970.

Bob Merrill 1921-

For biographical sketch and list of earlier songs see *Popular American Composers,* 1962.

———

With the collaboration of Charles Beaumont, Bob Merrill contributed eight songs to the motion picture *Wonderful World of the Brothers Grimm,* released in 1962. Among them were the title number, "Gypsy Fire," "Above the Stars" (also known as "Wilhelm's Theme"), and "Christmas Land." In 1964 Merrill wrote the lyrics to Jule Styne's music for the Broadway musical *Funny Girl,* starring Barbra Streisand as Fanny Brice. (The motion picture adaptation, also starring Miss Streisand, came in 1968.) For the Broadway musicals *Holly Go Lightly* in 1966 and *Henry, Sweet Henry* in 1967, Bob Merrill wrote both the lyrics and the music; both productions were failures. But in 1971 Merrill once again concentrated on writing lyrics by supplying the words to Jule Styne's music for the songs for the musical *Prettybelle,* which closed in Boston in its pre-Broadway run.

Theodore Metz 1848-1936

See *Popular American Composers,* 1962.

George W. Meyer 1884-1959

See *Popular American Composers,* 1962.

Joseph Meyer 1894-

See *Popular American Composers,* 1962.

Roger Miller 1936-

ROGER DEAN MILLER was born in Fort Worth, Texas, on January 2, 1936. When he was a year old his family moved to Erick, Oklahoma. His father died there when Roger was three. Since Roger's mother suffered from a serious illness, the boy was brought up by his aunt and uncle on a farm, while his brothers and sisters were dispatched elsewhere to find a home.

His uncle's intense poverty made it necessary for Roger to do farm chores at five in the morning, before walking three miles to school in time to make his nine o'clock class. "The school I went to," he recalls, "had thirty-seven students, me and thirty-six Indians. . . . During recess we used to play cowboy and Indians."

He remained in school through eighth grade while taking on whatever after-school jobs were available to a strong-shouldered boy. He worked as a ranch hand, herded cattle, dehorned cows, and rode bulls in rodeos. Somehow, despite his well-filled hours, he managed to learn to play the guitar, an instrument paid for with the money he earned by picking cotton. His inspiration and stimulus in turning to music had been Hank Williams, popular folk singer, whose records Roger had heard. At about this time Roger began writing his own songs. Then, as later, his subjects came from his own experiences: his hunger for the love of a mother; his need for affection; his loneliness and poverty. He entered talent contests in or near his home, from time to time managing to capture first prize. With this money he was able to buy a violin which he also learned to play without any lessons.

When war erupted in Korea, Miller enlisted in the United States Army. For a while he drove a truck in Korea, but before long was assigned to Special Services as a member of a hillbilly band entertaining troops. With this group he played the guitar, violin, and drums, and occasionally introduced his songs.

ROGER MILLER

Upon being discharged from the army after three years of service, Miller found a job as a fireman in Amarillo, Texas. He was fired two months later for being asleep when and after the fire signals rang. He decided that the time had come to try becoming a professional musician. He left for Nashville, Tennessee, with just enough money to pay for a night's lodging. He worked as a bellboy at the Andrew Jackson Hotel while peddling his songs to publishers, performers, and recording company executives (by now, Nashville had become a major center of popular music). The head of one company finally gave him a contract, but Miller's first three records were such failures that the contract was allowed to lapse. Ray Price then hired Miller to sing in his traveling show. More important still, Price recorded one of his songs, "Invitation to the Blues"—Miller's first success.

In 1958 Ernest Tubbs recorded Miller's "Half a Mind," a moderate seller. Two years later Miller began singing and recording his own songs for RCA Victor. Among his first releases were "You Don't Want My Love" (recorded also by Andy Williams for another company), "Sorry Willie," and "Teardrops." During 1960

other performers were also recording his songs: "A World So Full of Love" (written in collaboration with Faron Young), "A World I Can't Live In" (introduced by Jaye P. Morgan), and "Much Too Well" (written with Hawkshaw Hawkins).

Miller was now producing songs with unusual frequency, even though he was incapable of putting the music down on paper and was compelled to hire others to do this chore for him. (To this day he is still musically illiterate.) Miller himself recorded "The Moon Is High and So Am I," "It Takes All Kinds to Make a World," "Every Which-a-Way" and "When Two Worlds Collide." The last, written in collaboration with Bill Anderson, is of particular interest since it became Miller's first song on the list of leading hit songs of the month. In 1962 Miller recorded "Hitchhiker," "Hey, Little Star," and "I Catch Myself Crying," while other performers made recordings of "A Heartache for Keepsake" and "Golden Tear." The last recording Miller made for RCA Victor was "Lock, Stock and Barrel" in 1963. From then on he recorded for Smash Records, with whom he achieved his subsequent remarkable successes.

Since his songs, before he became affiliated with Smash, were not doing well commercially, Miller was forced to work as a drummer for the country-western star Faron Young. Miller then went to Hollywood to concentrate on dramatic acting; there for a while he was a member of an actor's workshop. The ambition to become an actor was permanently forgotten when some of Miller's early recordings for Smash began to make the grade. "Dang Me" and "Chug-A-Lug" in 1964 became top sellers, each achieving a sale of a million disks. "Dang Me" also brought Miller his first Grammys: as the year's best song, and as the best country and western performance. During 1964 he was particularly productive, and some of his successful songs of this period included "You Can't Roller Skate in a Buffalo Herd," "Feel of Me," "Got Two Again," "Hard-Headed Me," "The Willow Weeps," "I Ain't Comin' Home Again," "I'll Pick Up My Heart," "That's the Way It's Always Been," "Love Is Not for Me," among numerous others.

Bigger things were in store for Miller in 1965, a year in which he achieved wealth and international fame through "King of the Road." This was a typical Roger Miller ballad in that it reflected its creator's lifelong ability to maintain dignity and self-respect in the face of the most appalling adversity. "King of the Road" sold about two million records. Since Miller was drawing royalties as performer, lyricist, and composer, he earned $130,000 from his Smash recording alone. In time "King of the Road" was recorded by more than one hundred and twenty-five performers, and translated into about thirty languages. It received six Grammy awards, including those for the best single record of the year and the year's best country and western song. (In 1970 BMI presented it with an award for being one of the most often played country-western songs within the preceding five-year period.) Taking advantage of the enormous popularity of this number, M. Taylor wrote a parody, putting new lyrics to Miller's melody, entitled "Queen of the House," which became successful in Jody Miller's recording and received a Grammy as the year's best country-vocal performance.

Miller continued producing song successes. In 1965 he recorded "Engine, Engine No. 9" (reflecting his love of trains), "Kansas City Star," "One Dyin' and A-Buryin'," "The Good Old Days," "King of the Camp," "The Last Word in Lonesome Is Me," "This Town," and "Water Dog." In 1966 came "England Swings" (inspired by Miller's visit to London during his first trip to Europe) and "Husbands and Wives," both made successful in his own recordings. Miller also profited from a two-million-disk sale of "In the Summer Time" on an Andy Williams record. During 1966 Roger

Miller received six more Grammy awards, making him the recipient of eleven Grammys in two years, an achievement without precedent in the song business.

Between 1965 and 1967 four of Miller's albums each sold over a million copies: *Roger Miller/Dang Me; The Return of Roger Miller; Roger Miller/Golden Hits;* and *Roger Miller, The Third Time Around.* He was now a star of stars, selling out everywhere in public appearances in concert halls and nightclubs. He appeared as a guest performer on Andy Williams's television program late in 1965. The public response to his performance led NBC to star Roger Miller in a half-hour special on January 19, 1966. This in turn led to Miller's own regular weekly television show, beginning with the fall of 1966. That this series proved a failure—and that he was suffering a serious decline in popularity as a composer of songs and in public appearances—was the result of his overindulgence in illicit drugs, as Miller himself has confessed. "Before I knew it," he told an interviewer, "I was in a kind of snake pit. Pills were all I ever took." He quit drugs in 1969. "I decided one day I was going to be a man or a vegetable. . . . Only after my performance fell below par, my ability to concentrate declined, and my attitudes towards people began to worsen did I face the truth that you can't function with pills." Of the songs Miller wrote during the period he was addicted to drugs the best were "Walking in the Sunshine," "Little Green Apples," and "I Know Who It Is."

ABOUT:

Stambler, I. and Landon, G. Encyclopedia of Folk, Country, and Western Music.

Kerry Mills 1869-1948

See *Popular American Composers,* 1962.

Jimmy Monaco 1885-1945

See *Popular American Composers,* 1962.

Theodore F. Morse 1873-1924

See *Popular American Composers,* 1962.

Lewis F. Muir 1884-1950

For biographical sketch and songs see *Popular American Composers,* 1962.

It is now known that Muir was born in 1884, though the exact date and place are still unavailable, and that he died on January 19, 1950 (place unknown).

Alfred Newman 1901-1970

For biographical sketch and list of earlier songs see *Popular American Composers,* 1962.

After 1961 Newman continued to be a prolific contributor of screen music, as composer of background music and songs and in scoring; in background music and scoring he usually collaborated with Ken Darby. He served as musical supervisor and collaborated with Ken Darby in the scoring of *Flower Drum Song* (1961) for which they received Oscar and Grammy nominations; for *State Fair* (1962), a remake of the Rodgers and Hammerstein screen musical of 1945, he and Darby did the scoring; for *Camelot* (1966) he and Darby received an Oscar for the scoring. Other motion pictures in which Newman was involved were *The Pleasure of His Company; Counterfeit Traitor; How the West Was Won,* whose title song received the Western Heritage Award (lyrics by Darby); *The Greatest Story Ever Told,* the main theme from which, entitled "Jesus of Nazareth," was successfully recorded by David Rose and his orchestra and by the two-piano team of Ferrante and Teicher; *Nevada Smith; Firecreek;* and *Airport.* The scoring for *Airport* brought Newman his thirty-seventh Academy Award nomination.

Among Newman's songs for the screen were the title number and "Lullaby in Blue" from *The Pleasure of His Company* (lyrics by Paul Francis Webster), "Home on the Meadow" (Sammy Cahn) and "Wait for the Hoedown," "What Was Your Name in the States?", and "Raise a Ruckus," all to Johnny Mercer's lyrics, from *How the West Was Won.*

The letter to the editor of this book containing the above information was the last Newman was destined to write. It was dated February 8, 1970. Newman was admitted to the Cedars of Lebanon Hospital on February 10 where he died one week later, on February 17, with his wife and Ken Darby at his bedside. Private funeral services were held at St. Matthew's Episcopal Church in Beverly Hills on February 19. Newman was buried next to his mother in the Forest Lawn Cemetery in Glendale. The obituaries noted that during his forty-year career in motion pictures Newman had written for three hundred films and had won nine Oscars.

His widow, Martha (formerly Martha Montgomery), was his third wife; they had three children, two daughters and a son. By his two previous marriages Newman had two sons.

Chauncey Olcott 1858-1932

See *Popular American Composers,* 1962.

Roy Orbison 1936-

FAMOUS for his western and country music, both as composer and as performer, Roy Orbison was born in the oil-producing town of Wink, Texas, on April 23, 1936. His father began teaching him to play the guitar when Roy was six. During his boyhood, while working the oil rigs in Wink, Roy became the leader of a musical group, the Wink Westerners, which performed over radio station KVWC in Vernon, Texas. As singer and guitarist, he was chosen to represent Kansas at the International Lions Convention in Chicago when he was sixteen.

Orbison

ROY ORBISON

BMI Archives

In his late teens, Orbison entered North Texas State University where he majored in geology. There Pat Boone, already a recording artist for Dot in Tennessee, was one of his fellow students. Orbison's ambition then changed to becoming a recording artist rather than a geologist. In 1956 he induced Sam Phillips, an executive at Sun Records, to let him record one of his own songs, "Ooby Dooby." It sold three hundred thousand disks. This was followed by "Claudette" (Orbison's song tribute to his wife), recorded by the Everly Brothers.

Now on his way to success as a songwriter, Orbison left college to concentrate on music. Wesley Rose, of Rose-Acuff, Inc., a publishing house, became his manager and negotiated a contract for him with Monument Records. A handful of hits followed, all songs written by Orbison in collaboration with Joe Melson, and recorded by Orbison himself for Monument. Among them were "Only the Lonely Know the Way I Feel," "Blue Angel," "Running Scared," "Crying," and "The Crowd." Orbison's first album, *Roy Orbison's Greatest Hits,* was released in 1962. This was followed by *In Dreams* in 1964, the title number of which proved a hit as did several other

Orbison songs in the early 1960's, such as "Workin' for the Man," "Oh, Pretty Woman," and "It's Over," the last written with Bill Dees.

Roy Orbison made numerous best-selling records of songs by other writers. At the same time many prominent country and western performers were achieving major recording successes with Orbison's songs, among them Jerry Lee Lewis, the Everly Brothers, Buddy Knox, and Buddy Holly.

Since 1965 Orbison's principal record albums have been *There Is Only One Roy Orbison, Orbisongs, Orbison Way, Classic Roy Orbison, Very Best of Roy Orbison, Fastest Guitar Alive, Cry Softly Lonely One,* and *Roy Orbison's Many Moods.*

Orbison makes frequent public appearances in the United States, Canada, Europe, and Australia. When traveling in America or Canada he uses a thirty-foot mobile house for living quarters and transportation. In his offstage dress he favors the black suits and dark glasses which he wears in performance.

"What is the secret of Roy Orbison's success?" inquires Lillian Roxon in her *Rock Encyclopedia.* She continues: "He's not beautiful or even grotesquely arresting. His stage act is nonexistent. When singers all went hairy . . . Orbison remained pompadoured. A lone cowboy dressed in black with a pale face and perennial shades, he had an air that managed to be both sinister and old-fashioned. Yet he's constantly touring; he has the most fanatic fan clubs in England and Australia." There are numerous fan clubs in the United States as well.

In 1970 Orbison wrote the song "So Young," the melody based on a theme from the background music to the motion picture *Zabriskie Point.* He had introduced this number on Johnny Cash's television show where it proved so successful that it was added to the soundtrack of *Zabriskie Point,* heard over the final credits. Orbison recorded this num-

---

ber for MGM, to which label he had then recently transferred from Monument.

In 1970 Orbison made his debut as a motion picture actor in *Fastest Guitar Alive,* produced by MGM.

ABOUT:

Roxon, L. Rock Encyclopedia; Stambler, I. and Landon, G. Encyclopedia of Folk, Country, and Western Music.

Lee Pockriss 1927-

LEE POCKRISS, son of a businessman, was born in New York City on January 20, 1927. When he was twelve, Lee began taking piano lessons, but after the tenth lesson he left his teacher to study music on his own, which he did for many years. In 1942 he graduated from Erasmus Hall High School in Brooklyn; in 1948 he received his Bachelor of Arts degree from Brooklyn College where he specialized in English literature; and between 1949 and 1951 he was a graduate student in musicology at New York University. During these years he resumed formal music study. In 1948-1949 he was a pupil of Aaron Copland's and Leonard Bernstein's at the Berkshire Music Center at Tanglewood, in Lenox, Massachusetts. This was followed by four years of private study of composition with Stefan Wolpe, two more years with Tibor Serly, and one year with Max Persin. In 1950 he received first prize in a national contest for young American composers, sponsored by the American Federation of Music Clubs, for his *Little Suite* for oboe and strings.

While attending Brooklyn College, Pockriss played the piano in jazz bands at nightclubs, subsequently combining his piano playing with making arrangements and orchestrations. His first professional assignment as popular composer came in 1949 with the writing of special musical material for a show put on at the New York nightclub, the Latin Quarter. During the summers of 1951 and 1952 he wrote songs and special material for weekly revues produced at Camp Tami-

LEE POCKRISS

ment, an adult resort in the Pocono Mountains of Pennsylvania. In the fall of 1951 he made his first entry into the Broadway theater by writing music for the dance sequences in *Top Banana.* He performed a similar service for a second Broadway musical, *Jame,* in 1952.

He next devoted himself to television. Between 1953 and 1956 he wrote music for dance numbers and songs for the *Milton Berle Show,* and from 1953 to 1957 for the *Martha Raye Show.* During this period he also contributed music for two other regular television attractions, *The Show of Shows* and the *United States Steel Hour.*

His first hit song was "Catch a Falling Star" (words by Paul Vance) which Perry Como popularized over television and in a recording in 1957. This number brought its authors a Grammy. The same year Pockriss boasted another, though lesser, record success in "My Heart Is an Open Book" (lyrics by Hal David). "Big Daddy" (Peter Udell) was released in 1958. A year later three Pockriss numbers achieved record success: "What Is Love" and "Starbright" (both to lyrics by Vance), and "Sitting in the Back Seat" (lyrics by Bob Hilliard). In 1960 Pockriss's principal songs were "My Little

79

Corner of the World" and "A Kookie Little Paradise" (both to lyrics by Bob Hilliard) and "Jimmy's Girl" and "Itsy Bitsy Teenie Weenie Yellow Polka Dot Bikini" (both to lyrics by Vance).

Pockriss returned to the New York stage with a score for *Ernest in Love* which had a brief Off-Broadway run after opening on May 4, 1960. This musical was subsequently produced in Brussels, Belgium. Pockriss wrote the complete score for the Broadway musical *Tovarich*, based on the play and motion picture of the same name. It was produced on March 18, 1963, with Vivien Leigh and Jean Pierre Aumont, and achieved a modest run of 264 performances. Its leading songs were "Nitchevo," "It Used to Be," "I Know the Feeling," and "All for You." In 1970, with Carolyn Leigh as his lyricist, Pockriss contributed music for an adaptation of F. Scott Fitzgerald's novel *The Great Gatsby*.

Since 1960 Pockriss's leading songs to the words of various lyricists have been "Johnny Angel," "Dommage, Dommage," "I Haven't Got Anything Better to Do," and "Tracy." The last of these was written for The Cufflinks, a rock group formed by Pockriss, for whom he wrote songs besides serving as the producer of their recordings. "Tracy" placed on the top ten best-seller lists for six weeks in 1969. The second release by The Cufflinks was "Julie Comes Around," which in 1970 reached the top ten in England. As an independent producer Pockriss issued the record album *Jonathan Swift*, for which he wrote all the songs; it was performed by a new artist whose name provided the album with its title and whom Pockriss was promoting.

Pockriss's music for the screen includes the title song of *Stagecoach*; two songs for *Doctor, You Must Be Kidding* ("I Haven't Got Anything Better to Do" and "Walk Tall"); background music for *The Subject Was Roses;* and background music for *The Phantom Tollbooth*, an animated musical feature adapted from the best-selling children's book by Norton Juster.

Pockriss has also written music for numerous television commercials for Lever Brothers, Coca-Cola, Quaker State Motor Oil, Nabisco, and Post Company, among others.

ABOUT:
ASCAP Biographical Dictionary (1966).

Cole Porter 1892-1964

For biographical sketch and list of earlier songs see *Popular American Composers,* 1962.

———

While Porter was still alive there existed a good deal of confusion about the year of his birth because of his tendency to make himself a year younger. The correct date is June 9, 1892, not 1893 as stated in *Popular American Composers*.

Porter's last film score was *Les Girls*, in 1957, for which he wrote six songs. His last score for any medium was *Aladdin*, a CBS television special produced on February 21, 1958, where eight Porter songs were heard. *Can-Can*, the Broadway musical of 1953, was made into a lavish, beautifully produced and acted motion picture in 1960, starring Frank Sinatra, Maurice Chevalier, and Shirley MacLaine; the original score was supplemented by several Cole Porter numbers from earlier musicals. *Anything Goes* (1934) was revived Off Broadway in 1962, and produced for the first time in London in 1969. *Kiss Me, Kate* (1948) achieved a triumph when, on December 24, 1970, it became the first Broadway musical ever produced by Sadler's Wells Opera Company in London.

Porter's seventieth birthday was celebrated at the Orpheum Theater, in downtown New York, where *Anything Goes* was then being revived. Elsa Maxwell was mistress of ceremonies and the participants in the party included leading figures from New York's theatrical and musical life. A total recluse, Cole Porter refused to attend.

In the summer of 1964 Porter left New York for California as had been his custom for years. There he was operated on for the removal of a kidney stone. Though the operation was a comparatively minor one and no apparent complications set in, Porter died in the hospital on October 15, 1964.

Following his wishes, no public funeral or memorial service was held. His body was brought back to his native city of Peru, Indiana, where a simple service was conducted. As Porter had wanted, no memorial address was given; only a brief passage from the Bible was read. Porter was buried in Peru between his mother and his wife.

The Decline and Fall of the Entire World as Seen Through the Eyes of Cole Porter (1965) was an Off-Broadway revue in which the period spanning 1929 and 1945 was viewed through thirty-three Cole Porter songs. *Words and Music by Cole Porter* was a musical tribute to Porter telecast over NBC on November 25, 1965, starring Robert Goulet and Maurice Chevalier among others.

In July 1970 the American Ballet Theater presented the first production in forty-five years of a ballet for which Porter had written the music. This was *Within the Quota,* introduced in 1923 by the Swedish Ballet in New York and Paris. With new choreography and scenario by Keith Lee, and retitled *Times Past*—but retaining the original Porter score—the ballet did not make a forceful impression. "Mr. Lee's work is plotless," wrote Anna Kisselgoff in the New York *Times,* "but it is at its sharpest when there is a feeling that his characters are in fact fugitives from a plot. The Porter score—perhaps the first to contain what was called symphonic jazz—is not the most danceable and the choreography—simple in patterns but more complex in its steps—seems often to go against the music. When attitude and choreography come together, Mr. Lee comes up with some charming passages."

A definitive biography of Cole Porter, *The Life That Late He Led* by George Eels, was published in 1967. A picture biography of Porter, entitled *Cole,* edited by Robert Kimball, with a biographical essay by Brendan Gill, was published in 1971.

André Previn 1929-

For biographical sketch and list of earlier songs see *Popular American Composers,* 1962.

————

Since 1960 Previn has continued to be a productive and highly esteemed composer for motion pictures. The films for which he did either the scoring or the background music, or to which he contributed songs, include the following: *Elmer Gantry; One, Two, Three,* the main theme from which was made into the song "One, Two, Three Waltz"; *A Long Day's Journey into Night,* the motion picture adaptation of Eugene O'Neill's stage drama; *Two for the Seesaw,* whose score was nominated for an Oscar and which included the song "A Second Chance"; *My Fair Lady,* the scoring for which received the Academy Award; *Goodbye Charlie,* for which he also wrote the title song; *Inside Daisy Clover,* the song from its score "You're Gonna Hear from Me" being recorded by Frank Sinatra and by Barbra Streisand among others; *The Fortune Cookie; Irma La Douce,* whose scoring once again brought Previn an Oscar; *Thoroughly Modern Millie; Valley of the Dolls.* In addition, Previn wrote the song "Livin' Alone" for Julie Harris for the motion picture *Harper,* and the title song for *The Swinger.* For the above-mentioned songs, his lyricist was his wife Dory Langdon. They also wrote several songs not intended for screen productions but which were issued independently, including "Daydreaming" and "Control Yourself" (both introduced by Doris Day).

In 1967 Previn was appointed musical director of the Houston Symphony Orchestra in Texas. While holding this post he was also made musical director of the London Symphony Orchestra in England in 1968. He remained in Houston just two seasons, but continued to serve with the London Symphony with which his contract was extended to 1975. He has made several American tours with this orchestra and has also appeared as guest conductor with other major orchestras in both America and Europe.

Previn and Dory Langdon were separated in February 1969 and officially divorced in July 1970. Soon afterwards, Previn married the motion picture actress Mia Farrow, with whom he had twins, Sacha Villiers and Matthew Phineas. The Previns established permanent residence in England, near Dawes Green, an hour from London, where they occupy a modest house on ample grounds filled with trees and landscaped gardens. It is furnished with antiques.

Previn continued his career in popular music, following his separation from Dory Langdon, by forming a working partnership with the librettist-lyricist Alan Jay Lerner. Previn and Lerner wrote four songs which were interpolated into the motion picture *Paint Your Wagon*, released in 1969; this musical had been produced on Broadway in 1951 with a score by Frederick Loewe, most of whose songs were retained in the screen production. The four Previn songs were "The First Thing You Know," "The Gospel of No Name City," "Best Things," and "Gold Fever."

Previn made his bow as a composer for the Broadway musical theater with *Coco*, book and lyrics by Alan Jay Lerner. This was based on the later life of Gabrielle Chanel, Parisian dress designer (the role played by Katharine Hepburn). Though glimpses into Coco's past life (projected on a screen) are introduced, her story, as far as this musical is concerned, begins in 1954 when she is trying to make a comeback as a leading dress designer at the age

of seventy-one. She makes that successful return with the help of buyers from several American department stores. Except for Miss Hepburn's performance, the main interest in *Coco* lay not in the text but in the opulence of the costuming in a musical that proved to be an unceasing parade of fashion shows. The Previn-Lerner score was the work of skilled professionals and included several numbers of special interest, such as the title number, "Fiasco," "Ohrbach's, Bloomingdale's, Best, and Saks," "When Your Lover Says Goodbye," and "A Woman Is How She Loves." *Coco* opened on December 18, 1969, to an advance sale of over two million dollars. It had a Broadway run of 329 performances before going on tour.

Following her divorce from André Previn, Dory Langdon achieved success with songs for which she wrote both the words and the music and which were gathered in the albums *On My Way to Where* (1970) and *Mythical Kings and Iguana* (1971). She also wrote the title song for the television production *Say Goodbye,* in 1971.

Ralph Rainger 1901-1942

See *Popular American Composers,* 1962.

Harry Revel 1905-1958

See *Popular American Composers,* 1962.

Marty Robbins 1925-

A VERSATILE composer, Marty Robbins has produced rock 'n' roll, gospel, and blues, as well as the country and western music for which he is best known.

Robbins was born on September 26, 1925, in Glendale, Arizona, where he lived his first twelve years. Music played no part in his younger years. His main interests then were boyhood games and the movies—especially cowboy movies.

MARTY ROBBINS

In 1937 the Robbins family moved to Phoenix where Marty attended high school. He enlisted in the Navy in 1944, serving for four years. While on duty in the Pacific, he became interested in the guitar, which he learned to play by himself, and then used to accompany the songs he was creating.

After being released from service, Robbins returned to Phoenix with the hope of launching a career in music. He found some singing engagements in a local nightclub with a group organized and directed by one of his friends. Robbins concentrated primarily on singing country and western music, including songs of his own invention. Slowly his appearances in various nightspots grew more numerous and his reputation began to spread. Before the 1940's ended he not only had his own radio program but also a TV series called *Western Caravan.*

With the turn of a new decade, Robbins began receiving invitations to perform outside Arizona, mostly on the West Coast. He was given an opportunity to make some guest appearances with the Grand Ole Opry which proved so successful that in 1953 he was invited to become a regular member of the company; he soon became its star.

In the early 1950's Robbins signed a recording contract with Columbia. His first two important releases were his own songs, "I Couldn't Keep from Crying" and "I'll Go On Alone," in 1953 for which (as later) he wrote both the words and the music. He had another hit record in 1955, "That's All Right," following it in 1956 with "You Don't Owe Me a Thing," which a year later became a best seller in a recording by Johnny Ray. In 1956 he also wrote two blues numbers; "Singing with the Blues," which reached the top spot on best-seller lists in his own recording, and "Knee Deep in the Blues." In 1957 came "Please Don't Blame Me," and "A White Sport Coat." The latter recording was most responsible for attracting to Robbins the adulation of a teenage public; his recording appeared on the number one spot of every national poll of best-selling records. From then on, and through 1970, never a year passed without at least one or more of his songs on the best ten lists—"She Was Only Seventeen," "Stairway of Love," "El Paso," "Don't Worry," "Big Iron," "It's Your World," "Devil Woman," "Not So Long Ago," "The Girl from Spanish Town," "The Cowboy in the Continental Suit," "Begging to You" (the number one record in 1963), "Running Gun," "Hello, Heartache," "Another Lost Weekend," "One Window," "You Gave Me a Mountain," and "Camelia" among others. In 1970 "You Gave Me a Mountain" and "Camelia" received BMI awards for being two of the most frequently performed country and western songs within the preceding five-year period. In 1971 "My Woman, My Wife" received a Grammy as the year's best country song.

Marty Robbins also made the best seller record lists with songs by other composers. He has appeared frequently as a guest on major television programs and has given numerous public performances in America and Europe.

On August 1, 1969, while on tour in Ohio, Robbins suffered a heart seizure from which he recovered. An enthusiastic driver of racing cars, he was eager to determine whether this seizure would interfere with his hobby. He went for tests to the St. Thomas Hospital in Nashville early in 1970 where an examination revealed that two of the three main coronary arteries feeding blood to his heart muscles were completely blocked, and a third partially blocked. Open heart surgery was called for. From this delicate operation, Robbins has since recovered sufficiently to resume his career as songwriter and performer on a modest scale, and even to do some stock racing; on October 11, 1970, for the first time in two years, Robbins took the wheel of a racing car to enter the National 500 at Charlotte, North Carolina.

ABOUT:

Stambler, I. and Landon, G. Encyclopedia of Folk, Country, and Western Music.

Richard Rodgers 1902-

For his biography and list of earlier songs see *Popular American Composers,* 1962.

In 1962 Rodgers was appointed director of the New York Music Theater at the Lincoln Center for the Performing Arts in New York where annual revivals of outstanding musical plays and musical comedies are given. These revivals include some by Rodgers and Hammerstein.

No Strings (1962), Rodgers's first Broadway musical after the death of his collaborator, Oscar Hammerstein, received a Tony award as the season's best musical. Its principal songs were the title number, "The Sweetest Sounds," and "Nobody Told Me." Rodgers was also given an Emmy award for his background music to the television documentary series *The Valiant Years,* based on the life of Sir Winston Churchill.

The last of the Rodgers and Hammerstein musicals, *The Sound of Music* (1959), became a box office bonanza in its screen adaptation starring Julie Andrews, released in 1965, with an income esti-

mated at between a quarter of a billion to a half a billion dollars up to 1971. In 1965 *Cinderella*—which Rodgers and Hammerstein had written for television in 1957—was given a completely new production with a fresh cast on the CBS network. *Me and Juliet,* a Rodgers and Hammerstein musical from 1953, was revived Off Broadway by the Equity Library Theater in 1970.

The Rodgers musical that succeeded *No Strings* was *Do I Hear a Waltz?,* produced on Broadway on March 18, 1965. This was an adaptation by Arthur Laurents of his own Broadway stage play, *The Time of the Cuckoo.* Where in *No Strings* Rodgers had served as his own lyricist, in *Do I Hear a Waltz?* he used the services of Stephen Sondheim. The plot about a young American girl in a frustrated love affair with a married Italian, in Venice, Italy, proved slow-moving, for which other elements of the production provided little compensation. The best song in one of Rodgers' lesser scores was the title number.

While working on a new musical in 1969, Rodgers suffered a heart attack from which he recovered. He was able to attend an all-star production honoring the song era of Rodgers and Hart entitled *The Heyday of Rodgers and Hart* at Philharmonic Hall at the Lincoln Center for the Performing Arts on November 16, 1969. He was also able to work intensively and complete a new musical: *Two by Two,* a musical-stage adaptation of Clifford Odets's play about Noah, *The Flowering Peach.* When it opened on Broadway on November 10, 1970, most critics were generally agreed that the performance of Danny Kaye as Noah (in his first Broadway role in thirty years) far overshadowed all other parts of the production, including the score by Richard Rodgers, who here worked with Martin Charnin as his lyricist. Among the better numbers were the ballads "Something, Somewhere," "I Do Not Know a Day I Did Not Love You," together with "Ninety Again" and the title number.

Sigmund Romberg 1887-1951

See *Popular American Composers*, 1962.

Harold Rome 1908-

For his biography and list of earlier songs see *Popular American Composers*, 1962.

———

Though Rome's Broadway musical *I Can Get It for You Wholesale* enjoyed only a moderate success when it was produced in 1961, it contributed an important footnote to the history of American popular music. It was in this production that Barbra Streisand made her Broadway stage debut and first attracted attention to her uncommon talents as a comedienne and as a singer. The more important numbers from this Harold Rome score were "Have I Told You Lately?" and "The Sound of Money."

The Zulu and the Zayda, starring Menasha Skulnik on November 9, 1965, was a play with music rather than a musical comedy. For this, Rome contributed the words and music for about a dozen songs which were fully integrated into and were inextricable parts of the text. The best were: "Zulu Love Song," "Oisgetzaichnet," "Rivers of Tears," and "It's Good to Be Alive."

Rome also wrote the words and music for the musical-stage adaptation of the epochal motion picture *Gone With the Wind.* Renamed *Scarlett,* with Americans as director-choreographer, costume designer, and musical director—but adapted by a Japanese and performed by an all-Japanese cast—it was introduced in Tokyo on January 2, 1970, where it was a great success. This was the first time that Japan financed an American musical production, adopted American production methods, and enlisted the help of American talent in the presentation of a musical. Lehman Engel, the musical director of the production, described it as "one step short of an American opera . . . a bit more experimental than *West Side* Story or *Carousel.*" The details of how this production was put together were recorded by Rome's wife, Florence, in the book *The Scarlett Letters* published in 1971.

George F. Root 1820-1895

See *Popular American Composers*, 1962.

David Rose 1910-

See *Popular American Composers*, 1962.

Harry Ruby 1895-

See *Popular American Composers,* 1962.

Henry Russell 1812-1900

See *Popular American Composers,* 1962.

William J. Scanlan 1856-1898

See *Popular American Composers,* 1962.

Victor Schertzinger 1890-1941

See *Popular American Composers,* 1962.

Harvey Schmidt 1929-

HARVEY LESTER SCHMIDT was born in Dallas, Texas, on September 12, 1929, the son of a Methodist minister. Harvey attended the University of Texas where he majored in art, revealing in and out of his classes a natural gift for painting and illustrations. Music was a secondary interest and he learned to play the piano by ear. At the University he became a close friend of Tom Jones, who specialized in stage direction and aspired to a career in the professional theater. Jones aroused Schmidt's interest in the musical stage. In 1951 they collaborated on a college show, *Hippsy-Boo,* Schmidt contributing the music for the title number, and Tom Jones writing the sketches. They continued to work together after that, with Jones writing lyrics

HARVEY SCHMIDT

Bruce W. Stark

to Schmidt's music for a number of songs, and for the score of another college show, *Time Staggers On.*

In 1952 Schmidt was graduated from the University of Texas with the degree of Bachelor of Fine Arts. He was then drafted into the Army and sent to El Paso, Texas, where he painted latrine signs for the Field Artillery. His collaborator, Tom Jones, also drafted after graduation, was stationed in Baltimore where he was assigned to write reports for the Counter-Intelligence Corps. The two men maintained their friendship and their collaboration by mail, in time accumulating an impressive repertory of popular songs.

Following his release from service, Tom Jones went to New York where he directed a nightclub act starring Tom Poston and Gerry Matthews. Schmidt followed Jones to New York, where for a while he was a commercial artist. With Jones as his lyricist, Schmidt wrote music for a number of songs featured in a nightclub revue, *Demi-Dozen,* produced by Julius Monk. Jones and Schmidt also interpolated some of their songs in the *Shoestring Revue,* an unpretentious production that had a brief run. Among their best songs during this period of apprenticeship were "Mister Off Broadway,"

"The Race of the Lexington Avenue Express," and "A Seasonal Sonatina."

While writing songs, they often discussed different ways in which Edmond Rostand's play, *Les Romanesques,* could be made into a musical. Finally, in 1959, a fellow graduate of the University of Texas told them he would be interested in producing and directing such a musical at the summer theater at Barnard College, if they could compress it into one act. Schmidt and Jones complied with *The Fantasticks,* which was performed for the first time on August 3, 1959. One of those attending that night was Lorenzo "Lore" Noto, a young producer in search of a vehicle. He saw possibilities in this one-act musical and prevailed on its authors to expand it to full length, promising to present it Off Broadway. It took the authors nine months to finish this job. On an investment of $12,000, and with a cast of eight, *The Fantasticks* opened at the Sullivan Street Playhouse in New York on May 3, 1960. The reviews, damning the production with faint praise, were hardly of the kind to bring queues to the box office. A minority report, however, came from Henry Hewes of the *Saturday Review* who called it "one of the happiest Off-Broadway events in a season that has been happier off Broadway than on. . . . Jones and Schmidt have worked with professional expertness equaling the best Broadway has to offer with a degree of artistic taste that Broadway seldom attains anywhere."

The Fantasticks had all the earmarks of a failure. It was ready to bring down the final curtain after its second month when there took place a change of fortune with few parallels in musical-stage history. By word of mouth the news spread that this was a production full of charm, warmth of heart, and appealing entertainment—original in both the writing and the production. The theater began filling up, and it was not long before losses were turning into profits. After receiving the Vernon Price Award as the outstanding Off-Broadway production of the season, it continued drawing capacity houses for over ten years. During its seemingly interminable New York run, it was given over one thousand productions throughout the United States (in professional, stock, and amateur presentations) and, professionally, in Europe, the Middle East, Africa, Scandinavia, Mexico, and elsewhere. It was seen over the NBC-TV network on October 18, 1964—the first time in American stage history that a television production, on tape, had to compete with the live New York performance. By the end of a decade in New York, the overall profit exceeded one million dollars (bringing in a return of 5,000 per cent to its investors). *The Fantasticks* went on to become a classic, just as one of its songs, "Try to Remember," has become a standard.

The text is a free adaptation of the story of Pierrot and Columbine in which two young lovers are separated by a wall because their respective fathers are convinced that the only way to make the young people want to marry is to put up a false front of opposition. This ruse works, particularly after the fathers connive to have a bandit attempt to rape the girl and be frustrated by the heroic rescue of the girl by her lover. Once the two young people discover they have been duped by their parents they break up—and once again the fathers set up a separating wall. But in the end, the young people are reconciled and romance triumphs.

Much of the delight of *The Fantasticks* lies in the simplicity with which the play is presented. A single set is used with the most elementary means employed to suggest props (such as a stick for a wall, or nighttime suggested by a cardboard moon attached to a pole, and so forth). "The simpler you do something, the better off it's going to be," said Tom Jones. The simplicity is carried over in the dialogue which is poetic rather than realistic, and in the action, which has an almost ingenuous, childlike kind of treatment and development.

Harvey Schmidt, with Joe Darion as his lyricist, graduated from Off Broadway to Broadway proper with two successful musicals: *110 in the Shade,* on October 13, 1963, which had a run of 330 performances; *I Do! I Do!,* on December 5, 1966, which remained on Broadway for 584 performances.

The first was N. Richard Nash's musical-comedy version of his own stage play, *The Rainmaker.* The background is a western state, with all the action taking place between dawn and midnight of a summer day during a drought. A stranger convinces the town he is capable of relieving the drought, that he is a "rainmaker." The rains do come by the time the play ends, but not before the stranger has fallen in love with the heroine, Lizzie, a shy, introverted, and plain-looking girl who has long since despaired of finding a husband. As Lizzie, Inge Swenson made her Broadway debut. Some of the play's best songs are assigned to her, such as "Love, Don't Turn Away," "Is It Really Me?" and, in a comic vein, "Raunchy." Two other distinctive numbers are "Everything Beautiful Happens at Night" and "Another Hot Day." Commenting on the songs, Henry Hewes wrote in the *Saturday Review* that they "sustain the simplicity and tenderness of the story."

I Do! I Do! is the first Broadway musical requiring only two characters (enacted by Mary Martin and Robert Preston). Like the play, Jan de Hartog's *The Fourposter,* on which it is based, the musical traces the history of a marriage, beginning with the wedding day and going through the vicissitudes of marital existence until the couple's old age, when they finally succeed in coming to terms with each other and with life. The principal male character, merely designated as "He," is a successful writer, whose increasing popularity (not only with his reading public but also with the ladies) causes many problems through the years. The songs are beautifully interwoven into the text, potent contributors to the sentiment and tenderness, the humor and pathos of the text: songs like "Together Forever," "I Love My Wife," "All Dearly Beloved," "A Well Known Fact," "Where Are the Snows?", and "Flaming Agnes."

In *Celebration,* seen on January 22, 1969, Jones and Schmidt reverted to the kind of offbeat theater that had won them renown with *The Fantasticks. Celebration* deserved a better fate at the box office than it met, for as *Time* magazine noted, this musical was "a charmer for sophisticates who have never quite forsaken the magic realm of childhood . . . one of those good things that come in small packages." Otis L. Guernsey, Jr., thought well enough of it to select it as one of the ten best plays of the 1968-1969 season in his theater yearbook. But the public rejected it. "Love Song," "Where Did It Go?", "Mr. Somebody in the Sky," "My Garden," and the title number were its principal songs.

Harvey Schmidt has not abandoned his interest in art. His drawings and paintings have been published in such leading publications as *Life, Esquire,* and *Fortune.* With Robert Benton as collaborator he wrote the *In and Out Book,* in which a new concept of the words "in" and "out" is wittily introduced.

ABOUT:
Green, S. The World of Musical Comedy (revised edition, 1968).

Arthur Schwartz 1900-

For his biography and list of earlier songs see *Popular American Composers,* 1962.

The Broadway musical *The Gay Life* (1961), with which Arthur Schwartz had revived his once fruitful collaboration with the lyricist Howard Dietz, was a failure. But the score boasted at least two memorable songs: "Who Can? You Can!" and "Magic Moment."

On October 17, 1963, a new Schwartz-Dietz Broadway musical opened: *Jennie,* starring Mary Martin as the famous actress Laurette Taylor. With its short run of eighty-two performances it was an even greater failure than *The Gay Life* had been. The text, describing Miss Taylor's unhappy marriage with a cantankerous drunkard, was more fictitious than factual. "The music may not represent one of the distinguished composer's major efforts," said Richard Watts, Jr., "but it is pleasant and tuneful, containing a number of charming songs." Among them were "Before I Kiss the World Goodbye," "Born Again," and "I Shall Look at You That Way."

In 1970 Schwartz and Dietz collaborated on a musical diversion called *It's Entertainment* which included some new material but also presented some of their most popular songs from earlier revues.

Jean Schwartz 1878-1956

See *Popular American Composers,* 1962.

Raymond Scott 1909-

See *Popular American Composers,* 1962.

Paul Simon 1942-

THE TEAM of Simon and Garfunkel (since the 1960's one of the most successful attractions the popular musical field has known) owes its fame not only to the quality of its singing performances, accompanied by a single guitar, but especially to the songs Paul Simon has written for the pair. Art Garfunkel is sometimes credited with making the vocal arrangements.

Paul Simon was born in Newark, New Jersey, on November 5, 1942, just three weeks after his future singing partner came into the world. Simon's father was a professional musician who played the bass viol in a radio orchestra. (He later made a profession of teaching remedial reading.) When Paul was a boy his family moved to Forest Hills, in Queens, New York, where

PAUL SIMON

he grew up only three streets away from where Garfunkel lived. They met for the first time in the sixth grade in P.S. 164 and were assigned to appear in a school production. They soon became close friends, their relationship cemented by their mutual interest in singing and their passion for rock 'n' roll. They spent many an evening listening to the songs broadcast over Alan Freed's radio program which had been so vital in making rock 'n' roll popular. Simon and Garfunkel, aided by Simon's guitar accompaniments, were soon performing the latest rock 'n' roll hits at various school functions and club dates. They were also beginning to feature numbers written by Paul.

They made a demonstration record of two of Simon's songs which brought them a contract from a small company by the name of Big Records. Their first release was "Hey, Schoolgirl," (lyrics by Garfunkel), a rock 'n' roll number. It did so well that Simon and Garfunkel received an invitation to appear on Dick Clark's rock 'n' roll radio program; in addition, they were given some bookings in which they were billed as "Tom and Jerry." Their next few records, however, failed to sell; Big Records went into bankruptcy. It seemed that the careers of Si-

mon and Garfunkel, each of whom was then only sixteen, were over before they had really begun.

Simon enrolled in Queens College, New York, from which he ultimately received the Bachelor of Arts degree. Garfunkel went to Columbia College, majoring for a while in architecture. They did not desert music or their partnership. By this time, their main musical interest had shifted from rock 'n' roll to folk music. During their sophomore year in college, they made random appearances at small nightspots in Greenwich Village.

Simon was in Paris during the summer of 1963 (where he made some solo appearances as an American folk singer). In 1964 he read of the murder of Andrew Goodman, who had gone to Mississippi from New York to participate in the drive to register black voters in the Deep South. Goodman had been Simon's fellow student at Queens College. The tragedy, therefore, had a deep personal meaning to Simon, in addition to its profound social implications. As an outlet for his emotions, Paul Simon wrote the words and music of "He Was My Brother." This was the decisive turning point in his career as songwriter. "I . . . reached the point of knowing I couldn't write dumb teenage lyrics," Simon later told an interviewer. "And I had just about finally decided that if I was going to be a failure as a songwriter, I would be a proud failure."

Tom Wilson, an executive at Columbia Records, was impressed by Simon's new folksong style and signed him up to make an album. Simon suggested that his former partner, Art Garfunkel, join him in making this recording. In 1964 Simon and Garfunkel completed their first album, *Wednesday, 3 a.m.*, performing half a dozen of Simon's songs together with other numbers. The album did not sell, but a disk jockey in Miami started playing one of the songs. The response was so encouraging that Wilson decided to issue the tune as a single, substituting rock 'n' roll instruments (including an electric guitar) for the simple acoustical guitar that had been used as the sole accompaniment in the album. That song—"The Sounds of Silence," words and music by Paul Simon—became the number one best seller in the country and the first million-disk sale for the singing duo. There were two other distinctive Simon numbers in the neglected album, the title song and "Bleecker Street."

Early in 1966 Columbia issued the second Simon and Garfunkel album, *The Sounds of Silence,* which included "I Am a Rock," a Simon song that has become a classic. This album sold a million copies, and so did their succeeding one, *Parsley, Sage, Rosemary and Thyme,* released later in 1966. Some of Simon's best songs are included in this latter collection, such as "Scarborough Fair/Canticle," "Homeward Bound," "Dangling Conversation," "A Simple Desultory Philippic," "59th Street Bridge Song" (sometimes also known as "Feelin' Groovy"), and "Seven O'Clock News—Silent Night." In this last number, "Silent Night" is sung over a background of radio or television newscasts on Vietnam, racial conflict, and other social and political problems besetting the world that evening.

Their ever-widening audience included not only record buyers but also concertgoers. Simon and Garfunkel began making extended tours of America and Europe in the middle of 1965 and appeared as guests on major American television programs.

In 1968 Mike Nichols was producing the motion picture *The Graduate.* He had heard and been profoundly moved by "The Sounds of Silence," and hit upon the happy idea of having Simon and Garfunkel sing some of Simon's numbers on the soundtrack as a background for the movie. They sang "The Sounds of Silence" and "Scarborough Fair," together with a new number they had recently written but which at that time still had no title. As "Mrs. Robinson" it became another Simon song triumph. Paul Williams, a record critic, said

of "Mrs. Robinson" that it represented "true rock creativity. . . . The song rides the hump between gentleness and force; the melody is delicate and the rhythm is hard; so the effect is ideal, in this case psychotic." The album of the film soundtrack not only became still another gold release but also captured a Grammy as the best original score for a motion picture.

Their next album, and their next million-copy sale, came with *Bookends,* also in 1968, which included such remarkable Simon songs as "A Hazy Shade of Winter," "At the Zoo," "Old Friends," and "Save the Life of the Child."

The year 1969 brought Simon and Garfunkel two more Grammys: for "Homeward Bound" as the record of the year (another million-copy sale); and for "Mrs. Robinson" as the best performance by a popular vocal duo group.

But their most successful record release of 1969 was *Bridge Over Troubled Water,* which achieved the million mark in sales on the day it was released, passing the six million figure by March of 1971. The song "Bridge Over Troubled Water" became an extraordinary hit as did "Cecilia," also sung in this album. Other numbers in the album included "Why Don't You Write Me?," "Baby Driver," "The Boxer," and "The Only Living Boy in New York." With *Bridge Over Troubled Water* Simon and Garfunkel became the first American popular performing artists to achieve gold disks for each one of their first six albums. As a single, "Cecilia" was their fourth such to get a gold disk.

"Bridge Over Troubled Water" received five Grammy awards in 1971: as the record of the year (in recordings by Simon and Garfunkel); as the song of the year; as the best arrangement accompanying singers; as the best contemporary song; and as the best engineered recording.

Reviewing *Bridge Over Troubled Water* for the New York *Times,* Don Heckman said: "Simon and Garfunkel continue to represent that rarity in the popular arts—talent that can appeal to wide audiences without sacrificing a whit of originality, complexity, skill or creativity. Quite simply, 'Bridge Over Troubled Water' is a stunningly beautiful song. Like all classic popular ballads it has the virtue of instant identity."

In his songs, Paul Simon is undoubtedly a voice for his times. His message, wrote Josh Greenfield in the New York *Times Magazine,* is "one of literate protest against the pangs of youth, the pathos of old age and the matter-of-fact hypocrisies of the middle age and the middle class in between." Simon's songs seem, continues Mr. Greenfield, "to have transcended the communications breakdown, bridged the generation gap, broken through the usual establishment and anti-establishment lines." Speaking of the performance as distinguished from the songs themselves, Mr. Greenfield said: "Their sound—a soft and cool tenor and counter-tenor madrigal-like harmony to the accompaniment of a single guitar—has been acclaimed by the modern 'B's' as diverse as Leonard Bernstein . . . and The Beatles."

The annual income of Simon and Garfunkel is estimated at about two million dollars. Two thirds of it goes to Simon, since he writes the songs. Simon maintains a modest two-room apartment overlooking the East River on the upper East Side of New York. Its unostentatious furnishings include, of all things, a hobbyhorse—a "useless luxury," Simon calls it. He told one interviewer: "Otherwise I don't like to waste time on food, clothing, shelter, possessions—I don't even own a car. I don't have much relationship to my money."

When working, he rises at about 9 o'clock in the morning and begins right after breakfast. "Once I start on a project I never let up; I pace about the living room. I look over the river. I play some licks on the guitar. Or else I'll just go off to the Cloisters and sit there and think." He works on the music first, then spends a good deal of time writing and polishing his lyrics. "I try to take an emotion or feeling I've had," he says, "and capture it in one incident."

In 1970 Art Garfunkel launched a highly successful career as a solo performer and actor. He was featured in nonsinging roles in the motion pictures *Catch 22* and *Carnal Knowledge.*

ABOUT:

New York Times Magazine, October 13, 1968.

A. Baldwin Sloane 1872-1926

See *Popular American Composers,* 1962.

Chris Smith 1879-1949

See *Popular American Composers,* 1962.

Ted Snyder 1881-1965

For his biography and list of songs see *Popular American Composers,* 1962.

———

Ted Snyder died in the hospital in Woodland Hills, California, on July 16, 1965, following an abdominal operation.

Stephen Sondheim 1930-

STEPHEN JOSHUA SONDHEIM has distinguished himself both as a lyricist for composers other than himself, and as a composer for his own lyrics. His family was prosperous; his father was a dress manufacturer and his mother a fashion designer, both highly successful. Stephen studied the piano for two years, beginning when he was five. His early academic education took place in such private schools as the Ethical Culture School, Fieldston, the New York Military Academy, and the George School. It was at the last-named place that he first attempted at fifteen, to write for the musical stage. He wrote the book and music for *By George,* a school production.

Sondheim

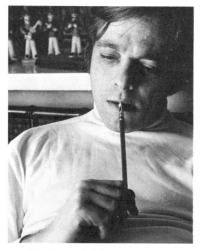

STEPHEN SONDHEIM

When Sondheim was twelve his parents were divorced. The mother and her son now made their home on a farm a few miles from the summer residence of Oscar Hammerstein II, in Doylestown, Pennsylvania. As a friend of Hammerstein's son, Sondheim was able to ask the famous librettist-lyricist for his evaluation of *By George,* which had then just been produced. "It's the worst thing I've ever read," Hammerstein told him. Then Hammerstein gave him a detailed explanation of what was wrong with the show. Sondheim says: "He went on for a whole afternoon about it. I guess I learned most of the things about writing lyrics in that afternoon: twenty-five years of his experience crammed into three hours. I gobbled it up." Sondheim continued to consult Hammerstein on everything he wrote up to the time of Hammerstein's death, and he does not hesitate to confess that Hammerstein's influence on his own development as a writer for the stage was decisive. "He got me into the theater, awoke a latent talent or a talent interest. . . . He'd been a second father to me since I was thirteen. Between the ages of thirteen and seventeen I was almost a member of Oscar's family. . . . I learned the fine points of lyric writing from Oscar. The fine points and the blunt points."

Sondheim gained valuable experience in the musical theater by working for Hammerstein. When Sondheim was seventeen, he spent his vacation typing scripts and doing other chores while the Rodgers and Hammerstein musical *Allegro* was in preparation. He also performed various duties during the rehearsals of *South Pacific* and *The King and I* at the same time he was attending Williams College, where he majored in music. "By the time I graduated," he says, "I was really ready for a professional career." At Williams (from which he was graduated in 1950) he wrote the book, lyrics, and music for two college shows. One was an adaptation of *Beggar on Horseback,* a 1924 Broadway comedy by George S. Kaufman and Marc Connelly.

After graduation from Williams College, winning the Hutchinson Prize enabled him to study composition for two years with Milton Babbitt, associate professor at Princeton University. Sondheim's professional career began in 1953 in television, when he worked as coauthor for the *Topper* series and wrote scripts for other television productions. In 1954 he wrote words and music for *Saturday Night,* a musical planned for Broadway. The death of its producer doomed this project. "I'm still proud of the songs, though. I wouldn't mind playing them right now for anybody," he has said. When his Broadway debut took place it was with incidental music to *Girls of Summer,* produced in 1956. During the same year he wrote scripts for the TV series *Last Word.*

One day Sondheim performed his score for *Saturday Night* for the playwright Arthur Laurents, who was then planning to write the text for a musical based on James M. Cain's novel *Serenade.* This production never materialized. Laurents turned to another stage venture, this time in collaboration with Jerome Robbins and Leonard Bernstein that eventually turned out to be *West Side Story.* A chance meeting between Sondheim and Laurents at a party gave Laurents the idea that Sondheim might be the right man to write the lyrics for Bernstein's music. When Bernstein heard some of Sondheim's lyrics, he agreed. *West Side Story* was produced on September 26, 1957. Sondheim suddenly found himself a collaborator in one of the most highly acclaimed productions in Broadway history.

Gypsy, starring Ethel Merman as Gypsy Rose Lee's mother, opened on Broadway on May 21, 1959. Once again Sondheim was the lyricist, this time with Jule Styne as composer; and once again he had a hit on his hands.

Successful though his first two maiden efforts on Broadway were, Sondheim was not happy serving merely as a lyricist. He had been trained in music; he wanted to be a composer as well. On October 29, 1960, the Broadway play *Invitation to a March* used his incidental music.

The first musical for which he wrote both words and music was *A Funny Thing Happened on the Way to the Forum,* which had its premiere on May 8, 1962. This was a bawdy farce, an old-fashioned burlesque filled with routines and gags even though the setting was ancient Rome and the text was loosely based on the plays of Plautus. Zero Mostel played the part of a slave trying to win freedom by getting a beautiful courtesan for his owner, although a warrior has priority rights to her. With rough and tumble humor that skirts the outer fringes of none-too-innocent merriment, the slave tries to convince the warrior that his courtesan died of the plague, as one of the other male characters acts the part of the corpse. The broad comic situations come thick and fast, culminating in a Mack Sennett-like chase. The audiences loved it. The show had an impressive run of almost one thousand performances on Broadway, received a Tony as the season's best musical, and was made into a successful motion picture in 1966.

In writing his score, Sondheim planned his songs (as he explained) to "provide periods of respite from the restlessness of the farce as one farcical situation piles upon another. . . . Though they're not used to develop character, they [the songs] still had to be written for a specific personality since the characters are all prototypes." The score begins with a rousing opening number, "Comedy Tonight," includes a fine ballad in "Love, I Hear," and highlights several humorous numbers including "Everybody Ought to Have a Maid" and "Lovely," the last a parody on sentimental ballads.

Sondheim's next venture on Broadway as a lyricist-composer was far less successful. It was *Anyone Can Whistle,* which opened on April 4, 1964, and closed just eight performances later. This was a satirical fantasy in which Arthur Laurents presented the thesis that in madness lies the sole hope for the world. Most of the critics agreed that the text failed to come off. Howard Taubman said in the New York *Times:* "In an attempt to be meaningful, *Anyone Can Whistle* forgets to offer entertainment." But Sondheim's score was by no means a negligible effort; its best numbers were the title song, "A Parade in Town," "Everybody Says Don't," "I've Got You to Lean On," "See What It Gets You," and "With So Little to Be Sure Of."

Sondheim suffered another failure with *Do I Hear a Waltz?* (March 18, 1965). This time he served exclusively as lyricist, with Richard Rodgers providing the music. But when Sondheim went back to writing his own music for his lyrics he emerged with another triumph in *Company.* Its official first performance on Broadway took place on April 25, 1970, when it was received with rhapsodic praise by the critics, capturing the Drama Critics and Tony Awards as the season's best musical, while Sondheim himself was the recipient of other Drama Critics and Tony Awards as the season's best composer and lyricist. The central character is a bachelor whose well-meaning friends are trying to marry off. The marital difficulties that enmesh the lives of his friends, however—combined with the fact that he is by no means denied a love life —serve to deter him. He remains a bachelor, even though in the end he has some doubts about the wisdom of his way of life. "It is not a musical in the conventional sense," wrote Henry Hewes in the *Saturday Review*. "The singing and what little dancing there is melt into one integrated continuity of action. The show is simply a collage of experiences. . . . Attention is also paid to the plight of young single girls who come to New York for freedom, but end up being unable to love a man who wants to live freely. . . . Indeed, so accurately does *Company* reflect New York life that the young in heart may want to rise up and scream about their anguish at the super-comfortable, superimpersonal environment our affluent fortyish swingers so unresistingly accept. . . . As a work of art it has remarkably distilled the essence of today's middle generation New York life."

The title song, "Another Hundred People" (describing the sad fate of lonely girls in New York), "The Ladies Who Lunch," "The Little Things We Do Together," and "Being Alive" are equally memorable for both their words and their music. As a composer, Sondheim has a sound respect for old-fashioned melody and neatly turned tunes that cling to the memory. As a lyricist, in the opinion of Arthur Laurents, he is the only one "who writes a lyric which could *only* be sung by the character for which it is designed, who never pads with unnecessary fillers, who never sacrifices meaning or intention for a clever rhyme and who knows that a lyric is the shortest of one-act plays, with a beginning, a middle and an end."

In commenting upon *Company* in *High Fidelity*, Gene Lees said that Sondheim "has grown enormously as a lyricist, and as a composer he is now without peer on the current musical stage. The *Company* score is absolutely first rate . . . the freshest . . . in years. . . . Sondheim's sense of musical (and theatrical) form is impeccable. He uses an interval of a falling minor third, based on the character's name, Bobby, as a motif throughout the show. It becomes a comment on, and a comment between, the other songs. The music is a departure from anything that's been done in Broadway shows . . . full of excellent songs. . . . This is a wonderful musical score, the one that Broadway has long needed, and my hat is high in the air for Stephen Sondheim."

In 1971 Sondheim wrote words and music for the Broadway musical *Follies*, text by James Goldman. With a cast headed by Alexis Smith and Gene Nelson it had its Broadway premiere on April 4 of that year. This, too, became a box office and a critical success, chosen by the Drama Critics and Outer Critics Circles as the season's best musical. This was a nostalgic and sentimental show, whose action takes place on the naked stage of an old theater about to be destroyed (presumably the New Amsterdam), once the auditorium for a famous revue (obviously the *Ziegfeld Follies*). The producer, Dmitri Weissman (Florenz Ziegfeld by another name) is giving a party for the former stars of his productions. Old friendships are renewed, old romances remembered as—with imaginative staging—familiar numbers from the old revues are revived, floating in and out of the production like faint shadows from a distant past. "Things move back and forth between the past and the present with the greatest of smoothness and ease," reported Richard Watts in the New York *Post,* "and you never have to bother with moody sadness. Not among so many proud and spirited people. . . . You can enjoy the sight of men and women relishing distant glories while delighting in a superb new show." Some of Sondheim's songs, both in the lyrics and in the music, recapture beautifully the sounds and styles of the popular songs of the past, and thus make their own contribution to nostalgia. Others are very much of the present-day musical theater. Memorable, indeed, are such songs as "Losing My Mind" (a torch song), the witty "I'm Still Here," the acidulous "Could I Leave You?", "Who's That Woman," "Broadway Baby," and "The Story of Lucy and Jessie."

Sondheim's home on East Forty-ninth Street in New York reflects his interests. The walls of his study are lined with bookshelves filled with phonograph records, which he collects as a hobby. He owns about ten thousand recordings of everything except opera. Besides an over-cluttered desk, this room contains recording apparatus and a piano over which hangs a collection of happy birthday songs written for him by Leonard Bernstein.

When he entertains friends, he uses his living room with its grand piano at one end. The furnishings also include such oddities as a skittle-billiard table, a verillon (which he says "looks somewhat like a box of musical beer glasses, and is"), a chess set, and walls literally covered from floor to ceiling with all kinds of games. Sondheim is a game addict who has managed to corral a veritable museum including The Games of the Goose, Transformation Cards, Loto Dauphin, a nineteenth century bicycle game, Skittle Billiards, Sky Jump, and a musical game in which players move notes and clefs on a sheet of music. "I just like to play games. I don't really care about winning or losing." The only game that fully absorbs him is anagrams, at which he is particularly adept. He himself invented about twenty games of his own, and has created what are described as "maddening, diabolical crossword puzzles" that have been published in *New York Magazine*.

Looking back on his creative efforts in the Broadway theater, Sondheim told Tom Burke: " 'Way back during *Gypsy*, I had begun to feel that the whole notion of Broadway musicals that depended on integrated songs—numbers that spring from the dialogue and further the plot—ought to be reexamined and perhaps changed. Though the tone of *Anyone Can Whistle* was off, the songs did break with tradition: they commented on the action instead of advancing it, and I think their relation to the book was excellent. In *Forum*, I'd already tried another break: songs that were respites *from* the action. In *Company* the songs are respites and comments."

ABOUT:

Ewen, D. New Complete Book of the American Musical Theater; Green, S. The World of Musical Comedy (revised edition, 1968).

High Fidelity, August 1970; House and Garden, July 1970; New York Times Magazine, May 10, 1970.

John Philip Sousa 1854-1932

See *Popular American Composers,* 1962.

Oley Speaks 1874-1948

See *Popular American Composers,* 1962.

Dave Stamper 1883-1963

For his biography and list of songs see *Popular American Composers,* 1962.

———

Dave Stamper died in Poughkeepsie, New York, on September 18, 1963.

Max Steiner 1888-1971

See *Popular American Composers,* 1962.

Joseph W. Stern 1870-1934

See *Popular American Composers,* 1962.

John Stromberg 1853-1902

See *Popular American Composers,* 1962.

Charles Strouse 1928-

CHARLES STROUSE was born in New York City on June 7, 1928, the youngest of three children. His father was an executive in the cigar-tobacco industry, his

CHARLES STROUSE
Friedman-Abeles

mother a trained pianist. Charles attended the city elementary and high schools, graduating from De Witt Clinton High School in 1944. He took his first piano lesson when he was nine but confesses that his musical interests at the time were limited. Piano study bored him until, while still in elementary school, he became a pupil of Abraham Sokolow, who for two years taught him how to play jazz and to construct jazz chords. Now that he could devote himself to jazz music, Strouse and his piano became inseparable; by the time he was fourteen he was an excellent jazz performer. He was thirteen when he started writing songs. His first was "Welcome Home Able-Bodied Seaman Strouse," written to honor his brother home on leave from the Navy during World War II.

Besides jazz, his main interests in high school (where he was hardly more than an adequate student) were athletics (especially baseball) and girls. He was also beginning to harbor vague yearnings to write music for the theater. These yearnings led him, upon graduating from high school at fifteen, to enter the University of Rochester where he could combine academic studies with musical training at the affiliated Eastman School of Music.

Attending the Eastman School represented Strouse's transition from jazz to serious music. He studied harmony, composition, and theory. Under the guidance of Bernard Rogers he completed several serious works.

After his graduation from the University of Rochester in 1947, he sent some of his music to Aaron Copland. Copland arranged for Strouse to get a scholarship to the Berkshire Music Center at Tanglewood, in Lenox, Massachusetts. There he was Copland's pupil and had some of his compositions performed for the first time. Strouse says he learned more about music from Copland than from any other teacher.

He earned his living at this time by taking a variety of assignments in the popular-music field. He played the piano in cocktail lounges and for the television series *The Goldbergs,* whenever the script required one of the characters to play; he did scoring and some original composition of background music for motion picture newsreels; and he wrote dance music for various ensembles and media.

During the summer of 1951, at Copland's suggestion, Strouse spent several months in France studying with Nadia Boulanger. He had an opportunity to play both his serious and his popular creations for her. It was Miss Boulanger who suggested to Strouse that his main talent lay in popular rather than serious music and who urged him to concentrate on the popular field. Notwithstanding this advice, Strouse continued to study for two years after returning to the United States, first with Arthur Berger, and then with David Diamond.

But even while studying with Berger and Diamond he was already devoting much of his time to popular music. This was due principally to his friendship with Lee Adams, a young writer for radio whom Strouse first met at a cocktail party in 1950. It was a number of years after this first meeting that they finally decided to work together, with Lee writing lyrics and Strouse music. Their collaboration came about in 1955 at Green Mansions, an adult summer camp in the Adirondack Mountains which put on stage productions each week and where Strouse had been given a job the previous year to write music. In 1955 he found a place on the entertainment staff for Lee Adams. All that summer they wrote songs and special material for the camp shows.

Following this summer experience, Strouse and Adams began to think seriously of promoting their careers as songwriters. They placed one of their songs in a Broadway revue, *Catch a Star*, which lasted just twenty-three performances following its opening on September 6, 1955. Some of the numbers Strouse and Adams had written for Green Mansions found their way into *The Shoestring Revue* in 1955 (for which Strouse was music director) and in *Shoestring '57* in 1956. Others were interpolated into *The Littlest Revue* in 1956 (basic score by Vernon Duke); *Kaleidoscope*, an Off-Broadway production in 1957; and in two London musicals, *From Here to There* and *Fresh Airs*. They also wrote the title number for the motion picture *The Mating Game*, which starred Debbie Reynolds and was released in 1959. By then they had about thirty songs published. One of Strouse's songs, "Born Too Late"—which he had written in 1958 with the lyricist Fred Tobias—became his first recording best seller, as sung by the Poni Tails.

Since writing, publishing, and placing songs in unsuccessful stage musicals was unremunerative, Strouse supported himself by writing music for a nightclub revue that George White produced at the Versailles (this time with Jack Yellen and Irving Caesar as his lyricists). He also played the piano for club dates, served as vocal coach, made vocal arrangements, wrote special material for Jane Morgan, Dick Shawn, and Carol Burnett among other performers, and served as rehearsal pianist for several Broadway shows.

In 1960 Edward Padula, a producer, was planning a Broadway musical satirizing rock 'n' roll and the adulation of teen-agers for a rock 'n' roll star like Elvis Presley. Having heard the Strouse-Adams songs in *Shoestring '57* he asked them to contribute a score for his show that could be used at auditions to raise money for the production. For a salary of one hundred dollars a month, Strouse and Adams wrote over forty songs which they performed for possible backers at seventy-five auditions. In time, Goddard Lieberson, president of Columbia Records, became interested in the production and arranged for its financing. Of the forty or more songs Strouse and Adams had written for the various auditions, only three were used in the actual production—*Bye Bye Birdie*—by the time it reached Broadway on April 4, 1960.

Bye Bye Birdie captured the hearts of both critics and audiences. The show abounded in vitality, excitement, and the exuberance of youth. "Everything about the musical was filled with a kind of affectionate freshness that we have seldom encountered since Mr. Rodgers collaborated with Mr. Hart on *Babes in Arms*," wrote Kenneth Tynan. The satire on the Elvis Presley craze was knife-edged, as well as humorous and boisterous. John Chapman called *Bye Bye Birdie* "the funniest, most captivating and most expert musical comedy one could hope for in several seasons of showgoing." It became a solid box office attraction (running on Broadway for over 600 performances), won a Tony and the Outer Circle Award as the best musical of the year, and was made into a lively motion picture, released in 1963.

Though this was their first full-length Broadway score, Strouse and Adams revealed themselves to be true professionals with songs like "A Lot of Livin' to Do," "Baby, Talk to Me," "Kids," and "One Last Kiss." Strouse revealed that "our problem was to satirize a kind of music—rock 'n' roll—that was so new it was hard to maintain a perspective about it . . . and also to use the form for real musical value."

When Edward Padula projected his next musical, *All American,* he did not hesitate to call upon the services of the now experienced and successful songwriters of *Bye Bye Birdie. All American* started out as a satire on colleges, with Ray Bolger playing the part of a football coach come to Southern Baptist Institute of Technology to teach engineering. Somewhere along the way, in writing his text, Mel Brooks forgot his original aim to be satirical or humorous and ended up with a routine musical tailor-made to suit the talent of its star. *All American,* produced on March 19, 1962, was a failure (80 performances). The best it could offer was Ray Bolger in an ungrateful role and a few good songs: a rousing patriotic number, "What a Country!", a ballad, "Once Upon a Time," "Have a Dream," and "If I Were You."

Success (though only a modest one) returned to Strouse and Adams with *Golden Boy,* a musical that had a Broadway run of 569 performances following its opening on October 20, 1964. This was an adaptation of the play by Clifford Odets, updated by changing the principal character, a boxer, from an Italian-American to a Negro. Sammy Davis, Jr., starred as the boxer. Odets himself had planned to make the changeover from stage to musical, but he died before the job could be done, and this assignment went to William Gibson. Highlighted by impressive choreography (including one of a fight sequence), a text whose dramatic interest was sustained throughout, and a score that contained several distinguished numbers ("I Want to Be with You," "Can't You See It?", "Colorful," "Night Song," "While the City Sleeps," and "137th Street") *Golden Boy* was a welcome addition to the Broadway scene.

It's a Bird, It's a Plane, It's Superman!, which opened March 29, 1966, was an attempt to bring to the Broadway musical stage the characters and fabulous situations of the comic strip *Superman.* The musical was not intended to satirize the comic strip (as Otis L. Guernsey, Jr.,

noted when he selected this musical as one of the ten in his *Ten Best Plays of 1965-1966)* but was "played straight as possible in a good laugh at our secret longing for a hero who could solve all problems and defeat all enemies. The joke is not on Superman. . . . The joke is right where it should be—on us and our childish instincts."

This musical, however, failed to meet favor, and closed after just 129 performances. The Strouse-Adams score was so well integrated into the text that few of its numbers stand out prominently from its context, unless it be "You've Got What I Need" or "Doing Good."

It was four years before Strouse and Adams returned to Broadway. When they did it was with a runaway success—*Applause,* which inspired rave notices from the critics and had queues lining up outside the box office even before its official Broadway opening on March 30, 1970. Like the source from which it was derived (the motion picture *All About Eve* that had starred Bette Davis), *Applause* removed the outer glitter, gloss, and glamour of show business to disclose the behind-the-scenes ruthlessness, deceit, megalomania, double-dealing, and cruelty that motivate the lives of ambitious young performers. Betty Comden and Adolph Green wrote a strong script with what Clives Barnes described in the New York *Times* as "a welcome lovely cynicism about show business . . . preserved in the most astringent aspic. This is a musical play that is bright, witty, direct and nicely punchy." Lauren Bacall gave a stunning performance as a middle-aged star who is victimized by an innocent-faced, seemingly lovely but treacherous girl in her successful determination to become a star in her own right. Miss Bacall received a Tony, as did *Applause* itself as the best musical of the season. The title number (the inspiration for an exciting dance routine), "The Best Night of My Life," "But Alive," "Good Friends," and "One of a Kind" were the best songs in the score.

Strouse wrote the book, lyrics and music for *Six*, an offbeat production described in the program as "a musical trip." It opened Off Broadway on April 12, 1971, and closed soon thereafter. This musical got its title from the fact that it called for just six performers who, for about an hour, sing a variety of songs on such subjects as life and death, criticism, Adam and Eve, goodness, etc.

Besides writing for the musical stage, Strouse has done background music, and at times the title song as well, for several motion pictures, including *The Night They Raided Minsky's, There Was a Crooked Man,* and *Bonnie and Clyde.*

In 1963 Strouse married Barbara Simon, a dancer. They have two sons (one born in 1966, the other in 1968) and make their home in an apartment on West Fifty-seventh Street, a stone's throw from Carnegie Hall. In partnership with Edwin H. Morris, Strouse founded his own music publishing house, Barbara Music, in 1971.

ABOUT:

Ewen, D. New Complete Book of the American Musical Theater; Green, S. The World of Musical Comedy (revised edition, 1968).

Jule Styne 1905-

For his biography and list of earlier songs see *Popular American Composers*, 1962.

———

Styne's greatest Broadway success came on March 26, 1964, when *Funny Girl* opened at the Winter Garden. Bob Merrill was his lyricist in this musical biography of Fanny Brice, played by Barbra Streisand in a performance that instantly placed her among the foremost stars of the musical theater. She helped make several Styne-Merrill songs notable successes, both inside and outside the theater, particularly "People," "Don't Rain on My Parade," and "I'm the Greatest Star." Other musical numbers of hardly lesser interest were "Who Are You Now?",

"You Are Woman," and "The Music That Makes Me Dance." *Funny Girl* was a box office triumph. It had a run of 1,348 performances on Broadway after which (in 1968) it was made into one of the most successful motion pictures in several years, with Barbra Streisand again in the starring role. For this performance she received an Oscar. Styne and Merrill wrote four new numbers for the motion picture adaptation into which Fanny Brice's tour de force, "My Man," was also interpolated.

Fade Out—Fade In (with Betty Comden and Adolph Green providing the lyrics to Styne's music) followed on May 26, 1964. This satire on Hollywood traces the career of a plain-looking chorus girl who, aided by accidents and coincidences, becomes a star. The part was played by Carol Burnett. This show would have done much better than its 271 Broadway performances suggest were it not for the fact that during the run Miss Burnett suffered from a back ailment which caused the show to close temporarily. When it reopened (with some revisions in the book and four new songs) it lasted only three months more. It was no secret that Miss Burnett was thoroughly unhappy with the musical; her withdrawal necessitated a permanent closing. A hardly more than average score was one of the defects of a production that had some excellent humorous episodes to recommend it. The songs included "Call Me Savage" and "I'm with You."

In *Hallelujah, Baby,* in which Leslie Uggams made her Broadway debut when the show opened on April 26, 1967, Betty Comden and Adolph Green were again Styne's lyricists. This musical was a panorama of Negro life in general, and show business in particular, over a sixty-year period. A unique gimmick in the text was the presentation of characters from the early 1900's who were not allowed to age as the years went by. The production suffered from a text that used stock characters and stereotyped situations in the presentation of racial problems. It was at its best in its staging, choreography, and vital performances by the principals doing some fascinating show-business routines. The musical numbers that evoked the spirit of each passing decade were "Feet Do Yo' Stuff" and "Smile, Smile, Smile" which reflected the frenetic mood of the 1920's, and "Another Day" the spirit of the 1930's. "My Own Morning," "I Don't Know Where She Got It," and "Now's the Time" were additional adornments to an above-average score. *Hallelujah, Baby!* received a Tony as the season's best musical.

Styne's next two musicals were failures. They were *Darling of the Day*, with E. Y. Harburg as lyricist, on January 27, 1968, and *Look to the Lilies*, on March 29, 1970, in which Styne worked with Sammy Cahn as lyricist. The first was an adaptation of Arnold Bennett's novel *Buried Alive;* the second was taken from the motion picture *Lilies of the Field*.

In addition to his songs for the Broadway musicals noted above, Styne wrote "Now" in 1963 (words by Comden and Green), a Civil Rights propaganda number adapted from the popular Israeli song "Hava Nagilah." It was introduced by Lena Horne. He also wrote the title song for the motion picture *All the Way Home* in 1963 (lyrics by Stanley Styne), and both the title number and "Musical Extravaganza" for the motion picture *What a Way to Go* in 1964 (lyrics by Comden and Green). These were followed by "Absent-Minded Me" (lyrics by Bob Merrill), introduced by Barbra Streisand in a recording, and "Time and Time Again" (lyrics by Cahn).

Styne wrote the music for several TV specials, among which are *Mr. Magoo's Christmas Carol* in 1962 and *The Night the Animals Talked* in 1967. In 1970 Styne announced he had become affiliated with Tele-Tape Productions to package and present musical shows for television, serving there both as composer and executive producer.

Styne's twenty-first musical was *Prettybelle,* an original musical with text and lyrics by Bob Merrill, staged by Gower Champion. It was scheduled for a Broadway premiere on March 15, 1971, but closed in Boston.

On June 4, 1962, Styne married Margaret Brown, an actress. This was his second marriage. His first wife was Ethel Rubenstein, whom he married on August 9, 1926, and divorced in 1951, after they had raised two sons. One of his sons, Stanley, has worked for the theater.

James Thornton 1861-1938

See *Popular American Composers*, 1962.

Harry Tierney 1895-1965

For his biography and songs see *Popular American Composers*, 1962.

———

Harry Tierney died in New York City on March 22, 1965.

Dimitri Tiomkin 1899-

For his biography and list of earlier songs see *Popular American Composers*, 1962.

———

In 1963 Tiomkin wrote the background music and did the scoring for the motion picture *35 Days at Peking,* for which he received an Academy Award nomination. Out of this score came "So Little Time" (lyrics by Paul Francis Webster), which Andy Williams introduced on the soundtrack of the movie and recorded successfully. "A Heart Must Learn to Cry" (lyrics by Paul Francis Webster) came from the motion picture *36 Hours,* released in 1965. In 1964 Tiomkin was once again nominated for an Academy Award, this time for the score of the motion picture *The Fall of the Roman Empire.* For this production he wrote, with Webster as lyricist, the song "The Fall of Love." During the same year Tiomkin scored the music for the motion picture *Circus World,* whose title song (lyrics by Washington) was nominated for an Academy Award. In 1970 Tiomkin served as executive producer and did the scoring for *Tchaikovsky*, a Soviet-made film based on the life of the Russian composer, with Tiomkin's score adapted from Tchaikovsky's works. This motion picture was given its world premiere in Moscow on September 1, 1970, with Tiomkin attending.

Egbert Van Alstyne 1882-1951

See *Popular American Composers*, 1962.

Jimmy(James)Van Heusen 1913-

For his biography and earlier songs see *Popular American Composers*, 1962.

Van Heusen continued being productive and successful in the 1960's, with Sammy Cahn as his lyricist, writing songs for the screen, particularly title numbers. Among the motion pictures for which Cahn-Van Heusen have written songs since 1961 were *A Pocketful of Miracles, Where Love Has Gone, The Road to Hong Kong, The Boys' Night Out, Under the Yum Yum Tree, Papa's Delicate Condition, Charade, The Pleasure Seekers, Robin and the Seven Hoods, Thoroughly Modern Millie,* and *Star.* Van Heusen received his fourth Oscar (and his third with Cahn as his lyricist) for "Call Me Irresponsible" from *Papa's Delicate Condition.* Other successful songs from the above-named productions were "Let's Not Be Sensible" from *The Road to Hong Kong;* the title songs of *The Boys' Night Out, Where Love Has Gone,* and *Charade;* and "My Kinda Town" from *Robin and the Seven Hoods.* For the last three songs Cahn and Van Heusen received nominations for the Academy Award.

In addition to working for the screen, Cahn and Van Heusen wrote "Love Is Born," which Barbra Streisand introduced on records, "Everything Makes Music When You're in Love," and "September of My Years," which served as the title number for a Frank Sinatra record album that won two Grammys. In 1968 Cahn and Van Heusen wrote an original score for an NBC television special, *The Legend of Robin Hood.*

Still with Cahn as his lyricist, Van Heusen wrote scores for two Broadway musicals, which were unsuccessful. The first was *Skyscraper,* based on Elmer Rice's play *Dream Girl;* it was produced in 1965. The other was *Walking Happy,* in 1966, adapted from the play *Hobson's Choice.* Both productions yielded hit songs: "Everybody Has the Right to Be Wrong" and "I'll Miss Her When I Think of Her" from *Skyscraper,* and the title number of *Walking Happy.*

A bachelor until 1970, Van Heusen in that year married the former Mrs. William Perlberg, a singer famous in the 1920's as a member of the Brox Sisters. The Van Heusens spend most of the time at their ranch in Yucca Valley in the Mojave Desert in California (while maintaining an apartment in New York and a house at Brant Lake, New York).

His passion has always been flying his own planes, particularly a Hughes 300 helicopter. Through the years Van Heusen gathered various ratings as a flyer, including that of Airline Transport (the top one in the aerial field), a commercial rating, and an instructor's rating in helicopters and rotor aircraft. Despite the last of these ratings he has never given a flying lesson. Other extramusical interests include collecting manuscripts of famous composers, photography, and the records of Frank Sinatra who has introduced and popularized so many of Van Heusen's songs.

Albert Von Tilzer 1878-1956

See *Popular American Composers*, 1962.

Harry Von Tilzer

Harry Von Tilzer 1872-1946

See *Popular American Composers*, 1962.

Fats Waller 1904-1943

See *Popular American Composers*, 1962.

Harry Warren 1893-

For his biography and list of earlier songs see *Popular American Composers*, 1962.

In 1967 Warren wrote the title song for the motion picture *Rosie*, with Johnny Mercer as lyricist.

JIMMY WEBB

Jimmy Webb 1946-

JIMMY LAYNE WEBB was born in Elk City, Oklahoma, on August 15, 1946, the oldest of seven children of a Baptist minister. His boyhood and youth were spent wandering from one Oklahoma town to another until the family settled in California. As a child Jim had started to learn to play the organ and piano. By the time he was eleven he performed on the organ in his father's church. By thirteen, he was writing songs. "Didn't We?" was one of the songs he wrote when he was seventeen; it became a hit several years later.

In 1966 he went to the San Bernardino Valley College for formal music instruction. Mental depression brought on by the death of his mother and his own confusion as to the direction his life should take in music combined to make him impatient with classrooms. When one of his professors advised him to concentrate on popular music he left college and, aiming to become a songwriter, went to Hollywood in a secondhand car he had bought for three hundred dollars. There he lived in a friend's apartment until he found a job in a recording studio for fifty dollars a week, transcribing songs for various performers. This assignment brought him into personal contact with Johnny Rivers, Richard Harris, Glen Campbell, and the Fifth Dimension, among other recording artists who were soon responsible for his meteoric rise to fame.

His first two hit songs came in 1967: "Get to Phoenix" and "Up, Up, and Away." The first reached the best-selling charts and was recorded by Glen Campbell, who received a Grammy for the best male vocal performance of the year. The other had been planned for a motion picture about a trip aboard a balloon which Webb had planned to make with a friend but which did not materialize. The Fifth Dimension recorded it in a release that received a gold disk. Trans World Airlines acquired the rights to use this song in its TV and radio commercials, and it captured no less than six Grammy awards, including that for the best song of the year.

The inspiration for both songs came from a frustrated love affair. The first time he saw the girl she was on the high school field officiating as a drill-team captain, "an all-American," he described her, "with long blonde hair and little canvas shoes. I worshiped her." One day in Los Angeles he began thinking of her and how she was out of his reach. His thoughts sprouted into "Get to Phoenix," which he completed in an hour and, some weeks

102

later, in "Up, Up, and Away" which he wrote in thirty-five minutes. The girl thus responsible for making Webb a songwriting success married another man in July 1968.

In 1968 Webb wrote a group of songs for Richard Harris to record in an album. It included a seven-minute number, "MacArthur Park," which (despite its length) was made into a best seller by disk jockeys; in five weeks' time the album sold over a million copies. Rick Sklar, program director of a New York radio station which was one of the first AM stations to feature this number prominently, said: "It's like a miniature symphony, and it has a certain sex appeal. Part of it is Harris's voice and the way he uses it. It lends itself to electronic treatment." Older people were partial to the lyrics, and younger ones to the strong beat in the music.

With a professional songwriting career just two years behind him—and having reached only his twenty-second birthday —Webb was already earning over $350,-000 a year, and owned his own publishing house (Canopy Productions) headed by his father who gave up the ministry to run the business. Webb loomed as the most talented new composer to emerge in the popular music of the late 1960's. His songs were in demand by famous performing artists (including Barbra Streisand, Frank Sinatra, and Sammy Davis, Jr.) who commissioned him to write songs especially for their use; and he was under contract to write music for the movies, the first of which was *How Sweet It Is,* released in 1968. He bought a palatial twenty-two-room mansion in Encino, California, which served both as his living quarters and as an office and rehearsal hall. He also indulged his passion for cars by acquiring two Corvettes, three Eldorados, a Camaro, and a station wagon.

Webb writes his own lyrics as well as the music, and prepares his own orchestrations. He never studied harmony or orchestration, but works by sheer instinct and, as he puts it, "by the seat of my pants." He explains: "One day, I called

up and said, 'Give me two trumpets, two trombones, and two French horns,' because that sounded like a nice even number—and I started writing for orchestra." He uses those instruments he feels he knows how to write for; at the same time he is always experimenting with what for him appear to be fresh combinations. In his melodies he prefers adhering to the traditional thirty-two-measure pattern. "I lean a lot toward traditional composers, some of the great . . . writers like Hoagy Carmichael and Jimmy Van Heusen. I don't believe in complexity for its own sake." Nevertheless his songs are fascinating in their often unusual harmonies and the way in which he introduces country music or the sounds of his southwestern background into his melodies. He feels that a good lyric should "basically be a poem. If people get the feeling, then the lyric is successful—whether they know what I'm talking about or not." About his work in general he says: "All the things I write about have existed in my life—they're reflections of things I've done."

The strongest musical influences on his creativity have been jazz and the classical music of such composers as Ralph Vaughan Williams and Peter Mennin. "I'm still convinced that the chord system is very much part of our scene," he says. "I may have written a few brief passages that might be technically defined as modal; but I'm basically a songwriter. . . . I am not a jazz man, but most of the musicians I use are jazz players. I like to structure some of my things with a jazz influence so that, say, a guitar player will come in and stretch out for sixteen bars before I go back to singing my song."

Late in 1968 Webb began recording his own songs. The first album was *Jim Webb Sings Jim Webb.* This collection includes his three big hits, "Up, Up, and Away," "Get to Phoenix," and "MacArthur Park." Other numbers were "I Keep It Hid," "You're So Young," "I Need You," "Our Time Is Running Out," "I Can Do It on My Own," and

"Run, Run, Run." Late in 1970 he recorded another album in which he sang his own numbers—*Jim Webb: Words and Music*. Its best numbers were "Sleepin' in the Daytime," "P. F. Sloan," "Love Song," and "Music for an Unmade Movie." In 1971 came *Jimmy Webb and So On*.

Besides the songs already mentioned, Webb wrote the following hits: "The Worst That Could Happen," "Paper Cup," "Wichita Lineman," "One of the Nicer Things," "I Don't Want This Modern Religion," "Gala," "Galveston," "Where's the Playground, Susie?" and "Evie." "Evie" received second prize among forty entries at the fourth annual festival of popular music in Rio de Janeiro early in 1970. Occasionally Webb touches on social themes, though this area has not yielded his best music. One such number is "The Yard Went On Forever," which had a ten-minute section about nuclear conflagration. This he confesses is "perhaps my least successful effort."

In 1970 Webb received the ASCAP award for "MacArthur Park" and the BMI award for "Get to Phoenix" as two of the country songs most often performed within a five-year period. In 1970 Webb contributed the songs to the Universal production of *Peter Pan*. In 1971 he did the scoring for the motion picture *Doc*. His first score for the Broadway musical stage, *His Own Dark City*, came in 1970. Webb also appeared as the star of a television special entitled "Jim Webb and His Friends."

"As he speaks to you," writes Leonard Feather, "you can take a little while to accustom yourself to the almost placid ease with which he accepts and talks about his successes. His face is mobile and sensitive. His hair is long; his figure is tall, his movements are casual but little. You sense in him the composure that overwhelming success can bring."

He dresses in the latest fashion (clothes are one of his main nonmusical interests). When dining out, he avoids expensive restaurants, preferring modest places specializing in Mexican food. His love of serious music has led him to compose some ambitious works including a concerto for cello and rock orchestra, a piano concerto, and a rock symphony.

ABOUT:

ASCAP Today, March 1970; Newsweek, December 23, 1968; Time, May 24, 1968.

Kurt Weill 1900-1950

For his biography and list of songs see *Popular American Composers*, 1962.

Weill's opera *The Rise and Fall of Mahagonny* (1930) received its belated American premiere (delayed thirteen years by copyright difficulties) in April 1970 in an Off-Broadway production. It lasted just a week. Previously, on November 9, 1969, Philharmonic Hall of the Lincoln Center for the Performing Arts in New York presented a concert of Weill's most popular American theater music, sung by an array of stars. "The skill with which Mr. Weill moved into the American idiom," reported John S. Wilson in the New York *Times*, "was constantly in evidence. He caught the airy, melodic style of the American musical, but he shaped it to his own ends, never letting his music grow soft or easy."

On April 11, 1971, Weill's 1936 antiwar musical *Johnny Johnson*, was unsuccessfully revived on Broadway. *Knickerbocker Holiday* (1938) was revived in San Francisco on May 11, 1971, with Burt Lancaster in the role created by Walter Huston.

Percy Wenrich 1887-1952

See *Popular American Composers*, 1962.

Charles A. White 1830-1892

See *Popular American Composers*, 1962.

Richard A. Whiting 1891-1938

See *Popular American Composers*, 1962.

Hank Williams 1923-1953

SOMETIMES described as the "hillbilly Shakespeare" or as "the king of western country music," Hank Williams has become almost a legendary figure. He was not only one of the most successful composers of country and western music but the first to emerge from a folk music area to achieve extraordinary success in the popular music industry.

Williams was born on a farm in Mt. Olive, Alabama, on September 17, 1923, but was raised in Montgomery. As a boy he was taught religious hymns and gospels by his mother, a church organist. To help support his impoverished family he sold newspapers and peanuts in the streets, but this did not prevent him from making music. When he was six he was able to play the organ well enough to accompany his mother's singing. He also was the youngest member of the church choir. At eight, he received the gift of a guitar which he learned to play so well without any instruction that in a few years' time he gained local recognition as a guitarist. In his twelfth year he won first prize in an amateur contest singing his own songs. Two years later he formed a band, Hank and His Drifting Cowboys, that performed at various local functions and square dances. It was given a regular spot over radio station WSFA, in Montgomery, Alabama, in 1937. This program became so popular that it was retained on the air for about a decade.

In 1946 he made his home in Nashville, Tennessee, where he did some recording and had a few of his songs published. One year later, Frank Walker, who had just formed MGM Records, signed him to a contract. About a year later, Hank and His Drifting Cowboys had their first hit record in "Move It Over." This was followed by "Mansion on the Hill" and "Lovesick Blues," which established Williams's fame and brought a fortune to the young record company.

HANK WILLIAMS

At about this time, Hank Williams married Audrey, a member of a group of performers calling itself the Caravan of Stars. Their son, Hank Williams, Jr., born in Shreveport, Louisiana, on May 26, 1949, ultimately achieved success as a singer, particularly in performances of his father's songs.

Hank and His Drifting Cowboys joined the Grand Ole Opry in 1949. Hit records now came in rapid succession. Two released in 1949 included his songs "Mind Your Business" and "You're Gonna Change," both of which reached the top ten lists. Four of Williams's songs in 1950 sold a million disks or more: "I Just Don't Like This Kind of Livin'," "Long Gone Lonesome Blues," "Moanin' the Blues," and "Why Don't You Love Me?" Six of his songs between 1950 and 1951 were made into best-selling records: "Baby We're Really in Love," "Weary Blues From Waitin'," "Hey, Good Lookin'," "Howlin' at the Moon," "I Can't Help It," and "Cold, Cold Heart." The last had a million-copy sale in a Tony Bennett recording in 1952.

Williams realized two other resounding successes in 1952 with "Jambalaya" (or "On the Bayou") and "I'll Never Get Out

105

of This World Alive." "Jambalaya" achieved best-seller status not only in Williams's own recording for MGM but also in one made by Jo Stafford in 1956; Brenda Lewis's rendition of this number for Decca was largely responsible for making her a recording star. "I'll Never Get Out of This World Alive," (written in collaboration with Fred Rose) achieved the number one place on the best-seller charts in 1952. Williams's other important songs were "Kaw Liga," once again written with Fred Rose, which earned an ASCAP country and western music award in 1952, "I Won't Be Home No More," and one of the most famous numbers Williams ever wrote—"Your Cheatin' Heart," written in 1952 and an immense success a year later in two different recordings, one by Williams himself, the other by Joni James.

Williams had for some time been suffering from heart trouble and, in addition, was mentally disturbed over an unhappy marriage. To escape from his misery, he resorted to overindulgence in liquor and pills. When his death came on January 1, 1953, it was from a heart attack while he was riding in his car in Canton, Ohio. Twenty thousand admirers attended his funeral services at the Municipal Auditorium in Montgomery.

Death did not end the vogue for Williams's songs, nor did it arrest the flow of his best-selling recordings. His numbers continued to be recorded by numerous artists and to reach the top ten lists. In the 1960's, MGM released several albums of Hank Williams's greatest hit songs recorded from fifteen-year-old tracks. As late as 1970 MGM issued a compilation of Williams's leading song hits in an album, *Life to Legend.*

Hank Williams, Jr., enjoyed substantial success singing his father's songs in concerts where he used an enlargement of his father's photograph as a backdrop. In 1964 the son's recording of his father's "Long Gone Lonesome Blues" was a best seller. The son's most important record album release was *Songs My Father Taught Me,* an album of Hank Williams's songs never recorded or published. They had been written at the end of the composer's life and had been left behind in a shoebox.

Williams's life story, *Your Cheatin' Heart,* was dramatized in a motion picture released in 1964. Hank Williams, Jr., sang his father's numbers on the soundtrack while George Hamilton played the part of the composer. The soundtrack recording became a best seller that year.

In 1961, when the new Country Hall of Fame was founded in Nashville, Tennessee, Williams was one of three chosen to be represented there. In 1966 Fred Rose Music, Inc., published several new Williams songs, including "I'm So Lonesome I Could Cry" and "A House of Gold." The latter received a Grammy as the season's best sacred recording. In 1969 *We Remember Hank Williams,* an MGM album, offered some of Williams's standards in performances by three members of The Drifting Cowboys among others. In 1970 Williams's "Cajun Baby" (as recorded by Hank Williams, Jr.) received a Grammy as the best instrumental performance of country and western music (by the Nashville Brass). It was also selected by BMI for an award as one of the most frequently played country and western music compositions in the preceding five-year period; a similar award was given by BMI for "Your Cheatin' Heart" and "I Saw the Light."

In its review of *Hank Williams: Greatest Hits, Vol. 1,* issued in 1967, *Hi-Fi Stereo* said: "Williams had, in his brief and turbulent hour, a magic gift for melody and homespun statement. His voice sobbed and cried with a plaintiveness that could touch and hurt. He may well have been one of the greatest white blues singers."

ABOUT:

Hemphill, P. The Nashville Sound; Williams, R. Sing a Sad Song.

Meredith Willson 1902-

For his biography and list of earlier songs see *Popular American Composers*, 1962.

Willson's first two Broadway musicals both became highly successful motion pictures. *The Music Man* (1950), which starred Robert Preston in his original stage role, came out in 1962; *The Unsinkable Molly Brown* (1962) starred Debbie Reynolds in 1964. Both utilized the basic stage scores. But in *The Music Man,* Willson wrote a new song for Shirley Jones ("Being in Love") while in *The Unsinkable Molly Brown* he created a new production number ("He's My Friend").

In 1961 Willson wrote "My State, My Kansas City Home" for the centennial celebration of the State of Kansas. Willson conceived the book, lyrics, and music of *Here's Love*—a Broadway musical produced on October 3, 1963, and based on the motion picture *The Miracle on 34th Street.* Its central character is an elderly gentleman who assumes the role of Santa Claus during Christmas and helps to spread a happy Yuletide spirit around him. He is employed by Macy's department store in New York as its Santa Claus, loses his job when the store psychologist considers him unbalanced, then gets his job back when his friends rally to his support. The spirit of Christmas penetrates two of Willson's best songs, the title number and "Pine Cones and Holly Berries." Other distinguished numbers were "Look, Little Girl," "Arm in Arm," and "My Wish."

Willson's next musical was *1491* in which Christopher Columbus is the principal character. Produced in Los Angeles in 1969, it was a failure.

Willson married Railina Zarova on March 13, 1948, a marriage that ended with her death in 1966. This was his second marriage; the first was to Elizabeth Wilson on August 29, 1920.

Septimus Winner 1827-1902

See *Popular American Composers*, 1962.

Jacques Wolfe 1896-

See *Popular American Composers*, 1962.

Harry M. Woods 1896-1970

For his biography and songs see *Popular American Composers*, 1962.

On January 13, 1970, Woods was struck and killed by a car as he stepped out of a taxi and was crossing the street to his home in Phoenix, Arizona.

Henry Clay Work 1832-1884

See *Popular American Composers*, 1962.

Robert Craig Wright 1914-

For his biography and songs see under George Forrest.

Vincent Youmans 1898-1946

For his biography and songs see *Popular American Composers*, 1962.

Youmans did not die in a sanatorium in Colorado as was reported in *Popular American Composers.* Hating hospitals, he defied his doctors and abandoned the hospital before his death to spend his last month in a suite at the Park Lane Hotel, in Denver. There, though deathly sick, he entertained visitors and sometimes left his rooms to go to parties and play his songs for the guests. When he was no longer capable of leaving his bed he kept his radio playing continuously. Lapsing into a coma he kept moving his arms as if conducting the performance.

Following funeral services at the St. Thomas Episcopal Church in New York, his remains were scattered over the waters near the Ambrose Lightship as he had requested.

His highly successful musical comedy of 1925, *No, No, Nanette,* was revived on Broadway on January 19, 1971, to rave reviews by the critics. In it Ruby Keeler (motion picture star of the thirties and forties) returned to the stage after thirty years' absence. Profiting from her delightful performance as Sue Smith, a greatly revised and updated text by Burt Shevelove, imaginative staging by Mr. Shevelove, and a considerable amount of nostalgia, humor, and interesting dance routines, *No, No, Nanette* proved a winner. Clive Barnes reported in the New York *Times* that it provided "a delightful, carefree evening," that it boasted "taste and imagination," and that it was "far closer to a musical of the twenties than anything New York has seen since the twenties, but it is seen through a contemporary sensibility." *No, No, Nanette* received four Tony awards in 1971 and an award from the Outer Critics Circle.

In 1970 a plaque was placed at Youmans' birthplace at 61st Street and Central Park West.

Victor Young 1900-1956

See *Popular American Composers,* 1962.

NEW BIOGRAPHICAL SKETCHES

Paul Anka
Burt Bacharach
Elmer Bernstein
Boudleaux Bryant
Johnny Cash
Cy Coleman
Bobby Darin
Antoine "Fats" Domino
Ervin Drake
Bob Dylan
George Forrest
Bobbie Gentry
Ernest Gold
Jerry Herman
John Kander

Mitch Leigh
Jerry Livingston
John D. Loudermilk
Rod McKuen
Henry Mancini
Roger Miller
Roy Orbison
Lee Pockriss
Marty Robbins
Harvey Schmidt
Paul Simon
Stephen Sondheim
Charles Strouse
Jim Webb
Hank Williams
Robert Craig Wright

INDEX OF SONGS, PRODUCTIONS, AND RECORD ALBUMS

Only songs and other compositions mentioned in the text are included in the index. In the case of works written by more than one composer, only those composers are noted who are subjects of biographies in this book.

Titles of songs are enclosed in quotation marks. Titles of all other works are in italics.

Index

Index

114

115

Index

Index

118

Index